OPERATION
BASALT

D1188742

OPERATION BASALT

THE BRITISH RAID ON SARK
AND HITLER'S COMMANDO ORDER

ERIC LEE

The
History
Press

Dedicated to all those who risked everything, and sometimes lost everything, in the fight against fascism – then and now.

Visit the website at **www.operationbasalt.com**

First published 2016
Paperback edition first published in 2017

The History Press
The Mill, Brimscombe Port
Stroud, Gloucestershire, GL5 2QG
www.thehistorypress.co.uk

British Library Cataloguing in Publication Data.
A catalogue record for this book is available from the British Library.

ISBN 978 0 7509 8421 8

Typesetting and origination by The History Press
Printed and bound in Great Britain by CPI Group (UK) Ltd.

CONTENTS

INTRODUCTION

A FOOTNOTE TO HISTORY

This book tells the story of Operation Basalt, a British commando raid on the tiny Channel Island of Sark in October 1942. At first glance, that seems a rather unimportant story, a footnote to history (and a rather small one at that). After all, this was a time when millions of men and women were engaged in a colossal conflict that spanned the entire globe.

Sark had no strategic value of any kind, a population of fewer than 500 people and 103 cows, and a landmass of 5 sq. km. One wonders what the German Army was doing there at all. Sark is one of the smallest of the Channel Islands, fiercely independent, with its own feudal system of government. So little was known about it in 1940 that the German soldiers sent to occupy it actually had to wire their superiors in Berlin to find out if Sark was even technically at war with the Third Reich.

Within a few weeks of this raid, the Wehrmacht would suffer a major defeat in the Second Battle of El Alamein, where the legendary Afrika Korps of Field Marshal Erwin Rommel would lose over 30,000 men. Churchill would later write, 'Before Alamein we never had a victory. After Alamein we never had a defeat.'

Just two weeks after the Sark raid, an even greater battle would begin in Stalingrad. Over the course of the next several months, an entire German army would be destroyed there. There would be hundreds of thousands of casualties on both sides.

In the larger frame of things, the commando raid on tiny Sark was surely insignificant. And yet for two men, this commando raid was hugely important. Those men were Winston Churchill and Adolf Hitler. From the moment the Germans seized the Channel Islands in 1940, Churchill was demanding from his generals a plan to liberate them. Churchill was a strong advocate of what were called 'butcher and bolt raids', which were aimed at making life for German soldiers anywhere in Nazi-occupied Europe as unpleasant as possible. In addition to terrorising the enemy, these raids were designed to gather intelligence that would be used later on when Allied forces would invade the European continent.

Churchill's personal interest in the raid on Sark was shown by his decision to invite the commando officer who led it to a private meeting in London a day after the raid. Churchill believed that small-scale raids would test German defences, keep them on their toes and compel them to keep large numbers of troops tied down in areas of no strategic significance throughout the war. If successful, the raids could also raise morale at home, which was essential following a string of bitter defeats for Britain and her allies.

Adolf Hitler also took an unusual interest in the Channel Islands. He had views about the loyalty of the Channel Islanders to the British Crown, a vision of which country the islands would belong to at war's end and even a plan to use the islands as a rest home for German working men and women. Hitler anticipated the October 1942 raid on Sark, or raids like it, even when his commanders insisted that the islands would not be targeted by the British. In a directive issued on 20 October

1941, a year before the Basalt raid, Hitler acknowledged that large-scale British assaults on the occupied Channel Islands were unlikely, but 'on political and propaganda grounds isolated English attacks must be expected at all times'.[1] He gave orders for the islands to be heavily fortified, each of them transformed into a *Festung* (fortress). He also demanded the deportation to Germany of civilians who might be security risks.

The news of the commando raid on 3 October 1942 moved swiftly up the Wehrmacht chain of command to Berlin and the German response to it affected the lives of everyone living in Sark – civilians and soldiers alike. But the German response went much further, culminating in Hitler's infamous *Kommandobefehl* (Commando Order), which was a death sentence for many Allied commandos, and a significant German war crime, raised in the Nuremberg trials.

Churchill and Hitler's interest in the Sark raid and its tragic aftermath make it worthy of our attention. But for me, what is really engaging about the story is the people; in particular twelve incredibly brave young men and one woman whose fate has been largely unknown until today.

After nearly seventy-five years, there is still much that is not known about the British commando raid on Sark in October 1942. As Ralph Durand, one of the first historians to write about the raid back in 1946 put it, 'The date and the fact of the landing are the only two points on which there is full agreement.'[2] He cited examples of rumours that reached Guernsey during the war:

> Of the local accounts that reached Guernsey none are official and none are based on the reports of eyewitnesses. One stated that ten men landed and went to the Bel Air Hotel, where they killed four men and took one man prisoner. Another, emanating from a German in sympathy with the British, stated that twenty Germans were killed or wounded and that one of the raiders was left a prisoner in German hands.[3]

That was back in the immediate aftermath of the war when memories were fresh and there were plenty of eyewitnesses still around. In the intervening decades, numerous accounts of the raid have appeared that often contradict one another. In this book I'm going to try to disentangle the facts from the myths and rumours that surround this raid.

This is the first book devoted entirely to Operation Basalt. Other authors have written histories of the commandos, or of individual soldiers, or of the occupied Channel Islands including Sark. This has meant that Operation Basalt is usually given only a few pages at most, and rarely put into the context of the history of the German occupation of the Channel Islands or the war as a whole. And while Hitler's Commando Order is sometimes mentioned, there is usually little effort to link it all up as a single story, as I have attempted to do here.

Some of those who have written about this raid seem keen to defend the local leaderships in the Channel Islands who were accused, in the years following the war, of collaboration with the Nazis. In doing so, they have failed to understand the importance of the raid, and in some cases have been quite dismissive of it. This does a disservice to the memory of the raiders, and to the truth.

The most important thing a historian can do is to tell the truth – and to let readers see the sources they have used. There have been too many cases of historians over-relying on secondary sources, which may not always be accurate, and which may have an agenda of their own. The best sources will be the ones found in the archives, particularly in the National Archives in Kew, in the local archives in Sark and Guernsey, and in memoirs, published and unpublished, by eyewitnesses to the events. Studying those sources in detail has allowed me to shed fresh light on what happened during and after Operation Basalt.

Through writing this book, I have had to touch on some wider issues, even though I don't necessarily come down firmly on a particular side in the various debates. I have had to address the question of the effectiveness of German Nazi propaganda, not only regarding the raid on Sark but also the far more famous examples, such as the firebombing of Dresden. I also needed to touch on the issue of the behaviour of some local residents under the very difficult conditions of occupation, focussing not only on the possible examples of collaboration, but also on the long-forgotten examples of resistance.

Unfortunately, so long after the event, not all facts can be ascertained, so where something is not known I have tried to make this clear. As a result, there are still quite a few unanswered questions about the raid on Sark, not least of which being the identities of the men who participated in it.

In all, the story of the British commando raid on Sark is one of great personal courage and daring, and the twelve men and one woman who played a role in it should be honoured and remembered. This work seeks to do just that and to shed light on the tiny Channel Island of Sark during the Second World War.

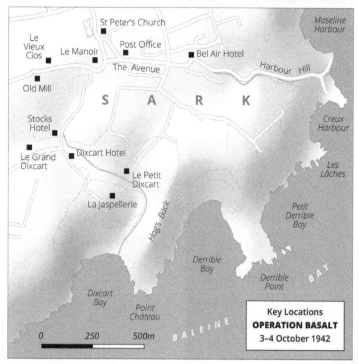

Key Locations
OPERATION BASALT
3–4 October 1942

(© David Wenk)

I

'DAS KLEINE PARADIES'

3 OCTOBER 1942

Peter Oswald had no reason to be particularly afraid that evening. The 35-year-old German corporal was on sentry duty on the tiny Channel Island of Sark. He paced back and forth, yawning, tired and bored. It had been an unusually hot day.

Oswald may have been thinking that he'd been having a very lucky war. After all, the German armies in North Africa were having a bloody time of it on the eve of the Second Battle of El Alamein, the first major German defeat of the war. And vast numbers of his fellow soldiers were stuck on the Eastern Front facing the beginning of a second Russian winter – one which would end with the disastrous battle of Stalingrad.

On Sark, they were much closer to German-occupied France than they were to England, and after more than two years of occupying the island, nothing remotely dangerous had ever happened to them. Not only had British forces never attempted to regain control of the Channel Islands, but the islands were among the very few parts of Nazi-occupied Europe that were off limits to Royal Air Force bombing raids.

By October 1942, the Second World War was about to take a sharp turn for the worse for the Third Reich. But on the Channel Islands, the German occupation had peacefully entered its third year. For some twenty-seven months, local

administrations in Guernsey, Jersey and Sark and the civilian populations they ruled had been co-operating with the
Wehrmacht in what became known as 'a model occupation'.

But not on Alderney, the third largest of the Channel Islands,
just 34km away from Sark. There, the Germans were showing a
different side to their occupation as they carried out what has
been called the greatest mass murder that has ever occurred
on British soil.[1] Thousands of forced labourers who had been
brought to the island died in Alderney's concentration camps.
They came primarily from the Soviet Union, but there were
also many French people, Jews, Italians, Spaniards, even one
Chinese man. In the final months of 1942, the deaths on
Alderney had reached their peak. As many as ten slave labourers a day were dying. The worst month of all, with the most
deaths, was October.

On Sark, the fourth largest of the Channel Islands, which
consisted of just 5 sq. km and with a civilian population of
fewer than 500, there were no forced labour camps and no
mass murders. Sark had a tiny prison that still stands today, but
it seems that it was never used. The horrors of Alderney and
continental Europe seemed very far away.

Werner Rang, a German medical orderly stationed in
Guernsey, visited Sark for three days that summer. Travelling
with his friend Karl Schadel, he was tasked with doing an inventory of medical supplies on the island and the two men stayed
in a bungalow during their visit. The inventory was a ruse;
Schadel was desperate for his friend to discover the lovely
island of Sark. A biographer of Rang writes:

> One fine evening he and Karl sat on the lawn of the bunga-
> low, eating fresh lobster and enjoying a few drinks which were
> still plentiful at the time. They were enjoying the evening sun-
> shine and the peace and tranquility that few places other than
> Sark can provide. The only sounds were the occasional cries
> of seabirds. The war and the horrors of what was happening

on the Eastern Front seemed a million miles away. Werner has never forgotten his colleague Karl's words on that evening. He described Sark as '*das kleine Paradies*' – a little paradise.[2]

Werner enjoyed his time on Sark so much that he managed to get transferred there, fell in love with a local girl and after the war settled down to live there. He lives there to this day, still married to Phyllis. And he was not the only German to be captivated by Sark's beauty.

Baron von Aufsess, the head of civil affairs in the German field command for the Channel Islands, wrote about the magic and beauty of the island. On a December 1944 visit to the tiny island of Herm, he looked out over the sea. He wrote:

> Sark lay before me. Bathed in golden light, the whole of the island was clearly visible and seemed like a model of the island of one's dreams; its tall cliffs fissured by deep bays and its upland plateau of lush verdant land etched in tapestried detail. I could hardly tear myself away from the sight …[3]

Later, he added: 'We passed near to Sark, which, with its girdling rocks, its deep bays and the causeway dividing Sark from Little Sark, must be the loveliest island in the archipelago.'[4]

Sark, like the other Channel Islands, was not only beautiful but also peaceful. Kurt Spangenburg, a sergeant in a machine gun battalion posted to Guernsey in 1940, felt safe there 'because the civilian population lived here, the British never made a bombing attack. I always said the Channel Islands were the best air raid shelter in Europe.'[5]

Sark in October 1942 was indeed unspoilt, beautiful and peaceful. But it was also heavily fortified, protected by minefields and barbed wire. The little building Peter Oswald guarded was deep inland, far from the cliffs. In the silence of the night, the only sounds he heard would have been the wind, the chirping of crickets and the snoring of his comrades.

Oswald's job that night was to guard five sleeping Wehrmacht engineers in a small building known as the Annexe, attached to the historic Dixcart Hotel. Until that night, the hotel was famous for just one thing: Victor Hugo slept there. Hugo lived for nearly twenty years in exile in the Channel Islands during the reign of Napoleon III. When he visited Sark, he stayed at the Dixcart Hotel.

As Oswald stood guard, counting down the hours until he was relieved, a Royal Navy Motor Torpedo Boat (MTB) specially fitted with silent engines was drawing up close to the island. On board were twelve of the best-trained and most experienced commandos in the British Army. One of them, the Danish commando Anders Lassen, was particularly expert at silent killing.

'OUR FOOT INSIDE THE DOOR OF THE BRITISH EMPIRE'

By the summer of 1940 the Germans were winning the war. To the east, the Stalin–Hitler pact had brought an end to the independence of Poland and the Baltic states of Estonia, Latvia and Lithuania. The unexpected alliance between the two totalitarian regimes had now lasted for nearly a year. Few people, least of all Stalin himself, expected it to end any time soon. In addition to dividing up Eastern Europe, the Soviets and Germans engaged in extensive trade and military co-operation. More than anything else, by ensuring quiet on the Eastern Front, the Soviets gave the Nazis a free hand to do as they wished in Western Europe, which they proceeded to do in May 1940.

In a matter of weeks, the Wehrmacht seized entire nations – with Denmark, Norway, the Netherlands, Belgium, Luxembourg and France having fallen. A new word had entered the world's languages: *Blitzkrieg* (lightning war). France's swift defeat at the hands of the Germans was a shock to the rest of the world's democracies, first and foremost Britain. Following the French collapse, the combined empires of Hitler and Stalin now stretched from the Atlantic coast of France to Vladivostok on the Pacific. With the Americans still out of the war, Britain and its empire were the only opponents of Germany still standing and fighting.

The evacuation of nearly 340,000 British and Allied forces from Dunkirk over the course of a week at the end of May and into early June 1940 meant that all that remained of the British Army was a defeated force that had struggled to get home. Though Dunkirk is now fondly remembered as one of Britain's proudest moments, it was Churchill who reminded the world that 'wars are not won by evacuations'.

The remnants of the British Army in the summer of 1940 were no match for the triumphant Wehrmacht. Britain did, however, retain its powerful Royal Navy and the world would soon learn that the Royal Air Force, whose fighter pilots Churchill would immortalise as 'the few', was still a formidable opponent.

In addition to those forces, Churchill personally pushed for the formation of special forces to terrorise the Germans who, now occupied nearly all of Europe. On 5 June 1940 he wrote: 'I look to the Chiefs of Staff to propose measures for a ceaseless offensive against the whole German-occupied coastline, leaving a trail of corpses behind.' The generals responded to the prime minister's colourful language by proposing a raiding force based on the irregular bands of Boer commandos who had fought against the British in South Africa. Churchill, who was himself a veteran of the Boer War, greeted the idea with great enthusiasm.

But in those terrifying June days, it seemed only a matter of time until the Germans would carry out Operation Sea Lion, the invasion and occupation of Britain. Had the Germans been able to pull it off, it is unlikely the Americans could ever have entered the war in Europe. Hitler's nightmare vision of a Thousand Year Reich may have become a reality. However, Operation Sea Lion was indefinitely postponed due to the inability of the Luftwaffe to take control of the skies over England. The fighter pilots of the Royal Air Force inflicted a stinging defeat on Hermann Göring's hitherto victorious airmen. But no one could have foreseen that in the weeks following Dunkirk. To any reasonable person, the war seemed to very nearly be over.

Though the invasion of England may only have been in the planning stages at this point, the Germans were able to carry out what must have seemed a dress rehearsal for the real thing when they decided to seize the parts of Britain they could reach: the Channel Islands. The islands, though considered part of Britain, are actually far closer to France. In 1940, many of the islanders spoke a local patois that was more French than English. But since the time of William the Conqueror, these islands had been part of Britain and loyal to the British monarchs.

The larger islands are Guernsey and Jersey, with Alderney and Sark following far behind. And there are several smaller islands including Herm and Brecqhou. In 1939, there were 50,000 people in Jersey, 40,000 in Guernsey, 1,500 in Alderney, and Sark had just 500. Sark, the fourth largest of the islands, is tiny. Including Brecqhou, which is just off its western shore, Sark is about 5 sq. km in size. Then, as now, Sark had no paved roads and no airfield. One got about the island on foot, by bicycle or horse-drawn carriage. It could only be reached by boat. Its main source of income was tourism and agriculture. Ruled by a hereditary feudal lord, Mrs Sibyl Hathaway, the Dame of Sark, it was a throwback to an earlier – much earlier – era.

In September 1939, with the outbreak of war in Europe, the local government in Sark ordered a complete blackout, which was not particularly onerous on an island with few electric lights. Most people used candles or paraffin lamps, and only the hotels had electrical generators. Nevertheless, two local men were given the task of patrolling the island to ensure that darkness was complete.

The following month, the Dame of Sark formed an Emergency Committee to take care of food and fuel supplies and other urgent matters. Mrs Hathaway appointed herself as president of the committee. She organised the women of Sark's British Legion to meet up in the afternoons to sew and knit articles of clothing for servicemen. A number of young men from the island volunteered to serve with the British forces as they had done during the First World War. One of them, Sub-Lieutenant Parkyn, did not survive the war.

Mrs Hathaway's Emergency Committee quickly found itself rationing petrol, which was used by the island's three tractors and its petrol-powered fishing boats. By January 1940, food rationing was introduced in Sark as it had been in mainland Britain. But few expected the war to reach the island. The experience of the First World War led most to believe that the fighting would be confined to the Continent. As a result, Sark's hotels and shops got ready for the tourist season as summer approached. In March, the British Government confidently assured travellers that the Channel Islands, including Sark, would be ideal for summer holidays in 1940.

At the insistence of the British Government, German and Austrian citizens throughout the Channel Islands were interned. There was only one 'German' on Sark at the time, Mrs Annie Wranowsky, who claimed to be Czech but carried a German passport. That passport was stamped with a large 'J', meaning that she was Jewish. As a German citizen, she was deported to Guernsey and was interned there, but released towards the end of June and returned to Sark.

For the first nine months of the war, the Channel Islanders felt like the fighting was something happening very far away, and would hardly impact on their lives. But in June 1940, the German Army broke through the French defences and reached the Atlantic coast. Their guns could be heard from the islands, and the islanders worried about what was coming next. The Dame of Sark wrote in her memoir:

> There was an ominous sign plain for all to see on 9 June when a dark pall of smoke rose sky-high from the coast of France and cast its shadow over the islands. The French were blowing up oil storage tanks: the enemy would soon be on our own doorstep.[1]

In London on 19 June, the British Government took the painful decision that the islands could not be defended. At that time, it was not even certain that England could be defended, let alone a handful of small islands just off the French coast. Churchill famously pledged that 'we shall fight on the beaches, we shall fight on the landing grounds, we shall fight in the fields and in the streets, we shall fight in the hills; we shall never surrender ...'

But not in the Channel Islands. Guernsey, Jersey, Alderney, Sark and the smaller islands were to be abandoned to their fate. British forces were withdrawn, including the tiny garrison on Sark, which consisted of a handful of men sent to guard the undersea telephone cable to Guernsey. The lighthouse keepers on Sark, as well as other Channel Islands, were collected by a special Trinity House vessel. This was the clearest evidence so far that things were about to change, and change dramatically, for the people of Sark.

Large-scale evacuations of civilians took place as well, including men of military age, a large number of whom enlisted to fight in the British military. Thousands left Guernsey and Jersey, and virtually the entire population of Alderney packed up and left as well. Mrs Hathaway announced that no matter what happened, she and her husband would remain on Sark. She was apparently quite persuasive. The authorities on Guernsey were informed that Sark would need no evacuation ship.

The British decision to demilitarise the islands was an important one, and the people who needed to be told this were the Germans. The government in London was busy with evacuations and sending final instructions on to the local governments in the Channel Islands to carry on and do their best. But they neglected to tell the German Army that there were no longer any British forces on the islands.

Friday, 28 June 1940 was a beautiful day with clear blue skies. At six in the evening, the Dame of Sark recalled:

We heard the intermittent drone of German aircraft and went out into the garden to watch three aeroplanes flying low over the island on their way to Guernsey. A few minutes later we heard the ominous explosion of bombs which were being dropped on St Peter's Port; but we were too far away to hear the machine-guns which fired on civilians in the streets, haymakers in the fields and an ambulance carrying wounded to the hospital.[2]

The Germans called this 'armed reconnaissance' and bombed the main ports in Guernsey and Jersey, killing and wounding large numbers of civilians. The Germans later insisted that they'd not been told about the withdrawal of British forces, and they mistook the lorries in the harbour for military vehicles.

The only example of anyone firing back reportedly came from the *Isle of Sark* mail boat. With Captain Golding in command, this little boat had been painted grey and equipped with four Lewis machine guns. The crewmen reacted instantly to the German bombing and kept up a continuous barrage.[3] As the Dame later wrote, 'Within half an hour the planes flew back over the sea to Sark, swooped down and machine-gunned our small fishing boats around the coast. As luck would have it their aim was faulty and no hit was scored either on the fishermen or their boats.'[4]

It is now generally believed that had the Germans known that the islands had been abandoned to their fate, and were demilitarised, they would not have carried out the bombing raids. The British Government did eventually inform the Germans of the demilitarisation of the islands through the good offices of the American Ambassador to the Court of St James, Joseph Kennedy. And according to some reports, the BBC declared the islands to be 'open towns' on their nine o'clock news programme on the day of the raid. But the message arrived too late to stop the 28 June raids.

Why the delay? It appears that the government was simply not keen for anyone to know, least of all the British public, that it was conceding a chunk of British territory and tens of thousands of British subjects without a fight. Both decisions, to abandon the islands to their fate, and then to not inform the Germans in time, did little to strengthen the bonds between Britain and the islanders.

For the Germans, the capture of the islands was a propaganda coup, proof that their unstoppable march through Europe would not end at the French shore of the English Channel. Taking the islands was seen as a dress rehearsal for the coming invasion of mainland Britain. But more than that, if the Germans could successfully occupy the islands and secure the co-operation of the islanders, it could be what they called 'a model occupation'. That might cause some Britons to rethink the need to fight to the bitter end, as Churchill was demanding. There were already plenty of British leaders, among them the Duke of Windsor, who would have preferred to reach an accommodation with a triumphant Germany in 1940 rather than continue with the war.

The day after the bombing of the harbours in Guernsey and Jersey, the first Germans landed by plane, met no resistance, and sat down with the local leaders in Guernsey and Jersey to give them their orders. Other Germans came over the course of the next few days, taking control without another shot being fired. For several days, no one seemed to notice Sark.

Meanwhile, in London, Churchill demanded that his army chiefs come up with a plan to take the islands back. He was convinced that with so few Germans having already landed, this could be done with a modicum of effort. He may have been right. But the same reasoning that led the British forces to withdraw from the islands in the first place convinced military leaders that they could not be defended. Every soldier was needed to defend the British mainland and could not be wasted on indefensible small islands just off the French coast.

The tiny island of Sark was not particularly important to anyone at the time.

Not very many local people took the opportunity, in the days before the German forces arrived, to be evacuated to England. Some did, among them the island's only doctor, who fled on a yacht just before the Germans arrived. The island's one Jewish family, the Abrahams, also reportedly fled. The Dame herself was certain that the Germans had no interest in Sark. At a meeting attended by many locals on a Sunday evening in late June, she said: 'The Germans are not coming here; there is nothing here for them to come for. I am having my granddaughter here; do you think I would have her here if I thought the Germans were coming?'[5] It was not an unreasonable thing to say, or believe. Sark had no strategic value to the British or the Germans. If the Germans were to come and occupy the island, it would only mean they'd be wasting valuable resources, and in particular trained fighting men, defending themselves. What would be the point in that?

At the end of June 1940, the islanders on Sark, the Dame included, knew very little about what was going on in the other islands as the Germans made a point of cutting the telephone cable that connected Guernsey to Sark. The Wehrmacht had taken the other islands, their aircraft had strafed some of Sark's fishing boats, but would they bother with an occupation of tiny Sark?

Despite the Dame's reassurances, some of the islanders were afraid. In the weeks following the German invasion of France, quite a few refugees from the Continent had reached the island and many were given help to continue on their way to England, and freedom. But the stories they told put fear into the hearts of the islanders. 'They all told us tales of the horrors of Occupation likely to create alarm and despondency,' wrote the Dame of Sark, 'for it was apparent that in the very near future we, too, would suffer the same fate.'[6]

The occupation of the larger Channel Islands, in particular Guernsey and Jersey, may have made some strategic sense.

They had a population of tens of thousands, and real economies that produced a considerable quantity of agricultural goods. The Third Reich also had a clear interest in controlling the passage of ships through the English Channel, and also in protecting the coast of occupied France. And there was the symbolic importance of occupying British soil, and having British subjects living under German rule.

But some of the Channel Islands, such as Brecqhou, were just too small to occupy. Sark seems to have fit somewhere in the middle, with its tiny land mass and population, too small to be of any real strategic importance but too large to ignore.

Part of the explanation for the decision to occupy the Channel Islands lies in the mind of Adolf Hitler, as was the case for so many of the decisions the Germans made during the war. Hitler was convinced that had the Wehrmacht not seized the islands when they did, they might have constituted a strategic threat to the Third Reich. He said in July 1942:

> If the British had continued to hold these islands, fortifying them and constructing aerodromes on them, they could have been a veritable thorn in our flesh. As it is, we now have firmly established ourselves there, and with the fortifications we have constructed and the permanent garrison of a whole division, we have ensured against the possibility of the islands ever falling again into the hands of the British.[7]

Hitler's views on the Channel Islands are known today because, during the course of the war, he was persuaded to employ a Nazi Party official whose job it was to sit at his dinner table and note down some of his pearls of wisdom. After the war, these were published in English as *Hitler's Table Talk*. At one of those meals, Hitler said that:

> The inhabitants of the Channel Islands which we occupy consider themselves as members of the British Empire rather than

as subjects of the King, whom they still regard not as King, but as the Duke of Normandy. If our occupation troops play their cards properly, we shall have no difficulties there.

Hitler had never visited the Channel Islands, and was apparently unaware of the fierce loyalty of the islanders to Britain. A visit to the war memorials on any of them, including Sark, would have shown just how many of the islanders had fought in the First World War on the British side and against Germany. He may not have known how many young men from the islands had evacuated to England in June 1940 in order to sign up to fight on the side of the Allies.

Hitler had plans for the islands after the war, which he was confident Germany would win. The Channel Islands were unlikely to remain under British rule, and would probably revert to being part of France. Two years into the occupation, he mused the islands could 'be handed over' to Robert Ley, the head of Germany's state-controlled labour front, which had replaced the country's trade unions after the Nazi seizure of power. 'With their wonderful climate, they constitute a marvellous health resort for the Strength through Joy [*Kraft durch Freude*] organisation,' he said. 'The islands are full of hotels as it is, so very little construction will be needed to turn them into ideal rest centres.'

As Lord Asa Briggs writes of Hitler:

> At times he seems to have been obsessed with the Islands. He was thrilled to have occupied a part of the British Isles and when his hopes of occupying the rest were dashed they did not matter less. He wanted them to be fortified for ever. For him there was to be permanence there.'[8]

John Nettles, the actor who played the Jersey television detective Bergerac, is also a historian, and in his recent book about the occupation of the Channel Islands, he writes that 'this obsession the Führer had with the islands and their fortification was lunacy, and indeed it was known as Hitler's *Inselwahn* or "Island madness"'.[9]

By the end of June, with the other Channel Islands already occupied, Sark held its breath. As Hitler himself put it on the last day of that month, 'Now we have our foot inside the door of the British Empire.'

3

FESTUNG SARK

The first German soldiers arrived on Sark on Wednesday, 3 July 1940, less than a week after they'd taken control of Guernsey. It was a sunny and hot day. Someone had spotted the Guernsey lifeboat heading towards the island and Mrs Hathaway was duly informed. She dispatched William Carré to meet the Germans. Carré was the island's seneschal, both a magistrate and the head of its parliament, known as the Chief Pleas. He was therefore the closest thing the island had to a head of government.

Carré was in no hurry. He reportedly stopped for a pint of beer at the Bel Air Hotel, at the top of Harbour Hill, and then strolled down to Creux Harbour to meet the boat when it arrived at midday. Normally, boats were met at the harbour by horses and carriages to take guests up to the top of the cliffs. But not today. The Germans were forced to climb up the steep hill to reach the inhabited part of the island. One of the fishermen reportedly said, 'Let's make the blighters walk!'[1]

Three German officers were on board the Guernsey boat, one of whom, Lieutenant Müller, remained on board. The two who came ashore were the German *Kommandant* from Guernsey, Major Dr Albrecht Lanz, and Dr Maas, a naval surgeon who came along because he spoke English. The fact that the Germans sent only three officers over by boat with no other soldiers shows how safe they felt. As had been the case in

Guernsey and Jersey, they were clearly expecting no resistance, and they met none. According to one account, 'the Germans took with them half a side of beef which was intended as a peace offering to the Dame of Sark'.[2]

As the two German officers walked up the hill to the little village on top of Sark's cliffs, a few islanders waited to see the newcomers and Major Lanz saluted them. But most seemed to have retreated indoors. Lanz believed Sark to be largely deserted, though he noted that curtains did seem to be twitching in some of the cottage windows.

While the Germans were on their way to meet her, Mrs Hathaway walked over to the island school to address the mothers who were waiting there. Once again, her role was to reassure. She told the mothers 'that most Germans were as civilised as Britons'.[3] These comments were to become a regular feature of her behaviour over the next five years under German occupation. They followed her earlier misplaced confidence that the Germans would not actually be coming to Sark in the first place. As she later put it, 'by assuming an air of cheerful confidence, which I was far from feeling', she steadied the mothers who had 'read of German brutalities in Poland'.[4]

But the Dame's knowledge of the Germans was limited to her experience in Weimar Germany. After the death of her first husband Dudley Beaumont in 1918, a victim of the Spanish flu, she had worked as a librarian for the YMCA in Cologne. She had no first-hand experience of the 'new Germany' under Nazi rule, and could hardly judge how 'civilised' they were. The Germany she knew was incapable of the 'brutalities in Poland' people were hearing about, and it was easy to dismiss those stories as war propaganda. She and the local people in the Channel Islands would soon find out how much Germany had changed under the Nazi regime.

She had already decided how she would react when the Germans arrived. She intended to be a proper host. She later explained that 'anyone visiting Sark, even an English tourist, is a foreigner and therefore should be treated as a guest who is entitled to courtesy no matter how tiresome he may be'.[5] In her view, the very worst a 'guest' could be was 'tiresome'.

Mrs Hathaway waited patiently at her official home, the Seigneurie, for the Germans' arrival. She told her husband, the American-born Robert Hathaway, the Seigneur of Sark, that they should 'take a leaf out of Mussolini's book' and move two chairs behind the desk at the far end of the drawing room. She said:

> It is a long room and they'll have to walk the whole length of it, which will give us a certain advantage. Besides, they'll have to walk up those few stairs from the hall and then turn right before they are announced, and that will also help us to look more impressive.[6]

This was to remain her attitude during the entire occupation, ever seeking to 'look impressive' and never to show any fear towards the Germans.

The German officers finally arrived, exhausted and perspiring from the long walk up from the harbour. She noted that when they arrived at the Seigneurie, Major Lanz and Dr Maas firmly wiped their boots on the doormat. She told her husband in a low voice, 'I know Germans. That is most reassuring. It is a gesture of respect to the house.'[7] Her maid announced their arrival, the officers entered, bowed and saluted. They gave the Hitler salute, but they did not exclaim 'Heil Hitler'. (The Dame later wrote that 'Heil Hitler' was never once said in her presence during the entire occupation.)[8]

To their great surprise, Mrs Hathaway replied to them in German, but she did not extend her hand to them. When they commented on the fact that she did not seem afraid, she asked them if there was any reason to be afraid of German officers. The German officers assured her that she had no reason to be afraid. She explained to them that she'd lived in Germany, and apologised for her imperfect command of their language.

The discussion that followed was quite a friendly one. She was convinced that the Germans were 'keen to make a good impression where people of what they called "*Kultur*" were concerned'.[9] They clearly included the Dame in this category, and they did make a good impression on her.

Mrs Hathaway and the Germans discussed books, the constitution of Sark and its place in the British Empire. She explained to the Germans, who obviously were not fully conversant with the legal system on the island, that though Sark was loyal to the British Crown, it was also entirely self-governing. Major Lanz was confused by this, and reportedly later sent a letter to the German Foreign Office in Berlin to find out if Germany was, in fact, even at war with Sark.[10] As Richard Le Tissier puts it, 'Right from the start Mrs Hathaway maintained a firm but polite attitude towards senior German officers, which was to stand her in good stead for the next few years of Occupation.' This remains the view on the island even today.

The officers presented Mrs Hathaway with their orders for the islanders. (It is not clear if they also delivered the side of beef they had brought over on the boat.) Those orders included an evening curfew, a ban on sales of spirits in pubs, all firearms to be handed over to the German authorities, limits on how far out fishermen could go, and so on. After receiving the orders, she invited them to lunch. Le Tissier writes, 'it was the Seigneur's traditional duty to entertain distinguished visitors'.

The officers returned that afternoon on their boat to Guernsey and the next day the occupation of Sark began. A German sergeant, Hans Hamm, led ten infantrymen up Harbour Hill. They occupied the Bel Air Hotel, where the seneschal had paused for a pint of beer the day before, and raised a large swastika flag. That flag was later put away as it too clearly marked the building in case of RAF air raids. Two of the men were posted to guard Creux Harbour, on Sark's eastern coast, the only place a ship could land, and two more would patrol the tiny island at night to enforce the curfew.

The Dame's husband, Mr Hathaway, noted the significance of the Fourth of July for an American. 'A hell of a day to surrender one's independence,' he said, 'and one I'll never forget.'[11]

Just ten days later, the first British commandos landed on Sark. They came as part of Operation Ambassador on 14 July 1940. Immediately after the Germans had seized the Channel Islands, and even before the occupation of Sark had begun, Winston Churchill demanded action from his army commanders:

> If it be true that a few hundred German troops have landed on Jersey or Guernsey by troop-carriers plans should be studied to land secretly by night on the Islands and kill or capture the invaders. This is exactly one of the exploits for which the Commandos would be suited.[12]

Unfortunately, the commandos were not yet suited for this sort of thing and this first raid was a debacle.

Operation Ambassador aimed to land a relatively large number of commandos on Guernsey. It was not a complete success. An entire landing party seems to have arrived on Sark by accident. According to Richard Le Tissier, the commandos who landed on Sark then:

> … were in a party of 140 men from No. 3 Commando and No. 11 Independent Company who were supposed to have landed on the south coast of Guernsey. The force was carried in two Royal Navy destroyers to Guernsey and several RAF Air/Sea Rescue launches were to transfer the troops from the destroyers lying offshore to the beaches. However, no adjustment had been made to the launches' magnetic compasses – one launch set off in the wrong direction and eventually landed on Little Sark. The small party proceeded ashore in silence, and after blundering around the La Sablonnerie area in total darkness and seeing no one, came to the conclusion that they were on the wrong island and returned to the launch. Fortunately, they

eventually found their parent destroyer and were able to return to the UK. No one on Sark, civilian or military, was aware of their clandestine visit.[13]

It is entirely possible that at this stage there were no Germans stationed on Little Sark. Little Sark, which is located to the south of the main part of the island, is practically a separate island from Sark itself, connected by a very narrow causeway called La Coupée. Later on, Germans would be based there, and would even have a permanent checkpoint at one end of La Coupée. But back in July 1940, they probably really were unaware that the British had landed.

Churchill was understandably frustrated and ordered that there be 'no more silly fiascos like those perpetrated at Guernsey'.[14] At this stage of the war, commandos were a very new concept and the idea that they could be landed in such large numbers was being tested. By late 1942, the Combined Operations Headquarters was focussed much more on small-scale raids.

The landing of men on the wrong island was not particularly unusual, as navigation was done without the benefit of the technology available today. A great deal depended on sighting the right island or lighthouse. The idea of the men wandering around Little Sark is also not surprising considering the almost total darkness that characterised Sark, then and now.

There are a number of such stories of unreported commando raids on Sark that the islanders tell today. Local historian Richard Dewe reports on sightings of British commandos on the west side of the island, and the possible cutting of a telephone cable to Guernsey there.[15] He also believes there may have been a British commando attempt to capture an Enigma machine held by the Kriegsmarine (German Navy) based at the lighthouse on the eastern side of the island.

Phyllis Rang, a local woman who became the wife of former Wehrmacht medical orderly Werner Rang, also remembers the night British commandos tossed gravel at the window of her father's house, trying to awaken him for some reason. She also reported that a girl she knew ran into British commandos elsewhere on the island one evening.[16] Actor David Niven, who was a liaison officer between the War Office and the commandos, described yet another unreported raid on Sark in his memoir. 'One party made a landing by mistake on Sark, which had no Germans on it at all,' he wrote. 'They were invited to the nearest pub by the locals.'[17]

It is possible that there were unreported British raids on the island, though there is no archival evidence of this. As a matter of course, the British Government did not make public any of these raids. The only reason we have a detailed and official British version of the October 1942 raid is because of what happened that night and the German reaction to it.

Sark, like the other Channel Islands, eventually became heavily fortified as a few hundred German soldiers were deployed there. Men were needed to lay mines and string up barbed wire, to man machine-gun emplacements and to patrol the cliffs at night. The island was turned into a fortress – *Festung* in German. The defences built in Sark were a small part of what became known as the Atlantic Wall. This 'wall' was an immense construction project consisting of concrete and steel barriers, barbed wire, minefields, anti-tank obstacles and ditches that ran from the Arctic Circle in Norway down to the coast of Spain. It was designed to withstand the inevitable Allied invasion of Western Europe, which finally came on 6 June 1944.

Because the Germans couldn't know exactly where the Allies would land, they fortified everything – pouring vast resources into fortifying the Channel Islands as well. Slave labour was employed in many places and many thousands gave their lives in the construction of these defences. An extraordinary amount of the construction work took place in the Channel Islands. According to one estimate, between 10 and 12 per cent of all the resources invested in creating Hitler's Atlantic Wall were spent in the Channel Islands.[18]

The vast over-investment of resources in defending territories that held no strategic value for Germany, such as Sark, did not go unnoticed in the Wehrmacht. While Allied air forces were pounding German positions in occupied France, Generalfeldmarschall Gerd von Rundstedt, among others, complained that some of the anti-aircraft weapons sitting unused in the Channel Islands could be put to better use elsewhere. Though Rundstedt was the Wehrmacht's commander-in-chief in the west, his advice was ignored.

The German soldiers stationed on Sark consisted primarily of men from 6 Company of the 319th Infantry Division, which had men stationed on the other Channel Islands as well. That infantry division, previously based in France, is the one that Hitler proudly relocated to the Channel Islands to ensure 'against the possibility of the islands ever falling again into the hands of the British'. (He neglected to note that it meant an entire division would not be available to defend, for example, France, or to beef up German forces fighting for their lives on the Eastern Front.)

That company on Sark included a heavy machine gun section, an anti-tank platoon and a light mortar group. In addition to the infantrymen, there were sometimes groups of engineers, including the unlucky men who found themselves billeted in Sark's Dixcart Hotel on the night of 3 October 1942. There were also customs officials who patrolled the island's cliffs at night. Overall, there seem to have been about 300 German soldiers on Sark, an island that had a population of fewer than 500 at the time.

Those German soldiers on Sark were occupied entirely with the task of defending themselves, and they had at their disposal three anti-tank guns, three flamethrowers, a light machine gun and hundreds (later, thousands) of mines, including S-mines (also known as 'bouncing Betties'). Those mines, first developed in Germany in the 1930s, were mass produced, with estimates that the Wehrmacht eventually had nearly 2 million of them.

They got their nickname because they would bounce and detonate at a height of about 0.9m. Unlike ordinary landmines, which would blow off legs, the bouncing Betties were designed to kill, and kill they did in vast numbers. Many thousands of them were used as part of the Atlantic Wall, with a large number of them deployed in the Channel Islands. The mines were laid on beaches and clifftops around Sark, in at least twenty-two separate minefields. At the time of the October 1942 commando raid, there were already about 1,000 mines laid. Following that raid, there would be many more.

The only beach that wasn't mined was La Grand Grève at the foot of La Coupée, the narrow isthmus that separates Little Sark from the main island to its north. That beach wasn't mined because the German soldiers liked to bathe there. Creux Harbour, the mostly likely place for an Allied landing on Sark, was defended with mines and other barriers and the Germans sealed off the tunnel connecting it with the road leading up to the village. They also barricaded La Coupée at night, with a number of sentries permanently posted there.

The commander of German forces on Sark for much of the war was Oberleutnant (First Lieutenant) Heinz Herdt. If German soldiers who were stationed in the Channel Islands may be considered among the luckiest men in the Wehrmacht, Herdt's luck was greater still. Born in 1915, Herdt trained to be a teacher but was called up to serve in the Wehrmacht in September 1939 at the outbreak of the war. He was selected for officer training and served with German forces in Poland and Belgium. He first arrived in Sark, commanding a company of infantry, in March 1942 and was given the title of *Inselkommandant* (island commander).

He was considered successful at his post, particularly in comparison to the previous *Inselkommandant* on whose watch soldiers accidentally burnt down the German headquarters at the Bel Air Hotel. That fire forced the Germans to move over to Le Manoir, a large granite building dating from 1565 and built by the first Seigneur of Sark, Helier De Carteret. It sits at the far end of The Avenue, just on the edge of the village. In June 1942, Herdt was back in Guernsey, but at the end of the summer, he began his second tour on Sark as *Inselkommandant*.

Herdt was well liked on Sark, and developed a friendship with the Dame. He would ride his horse around the island's lanes and along its cliffs. The islanders noticed how much shorter he was than the other Germans and nicknamed him 'Little Steve'. As Mrs Esther Perree remembers it, he got the nickname because one of the local men was called 'Little Steve' and islanders thought Herdt resembled him.[19] Herdt's friendship with the Dame of Sark would come in quite handy later on.

The only German soldier to die a violent death on Sark before the arrival of the commandos was the army doctor, found murdered in his bed. The Germans suspected the islanders. It was not an unreasonable suspicion, as they were an occupying power on British soil, and German soldiers everywhere else in Europe were being killed on a regular basis by partisans. The Dame of Sark insisted that could not be the case here. 'The islanders don't murder people,' she said, adding that 'there hasn't been a murder on Sark for hundreds of years.'[20]

It eventually turned out that a German soldier desperate to avoid being sent from the '*kleine Paradies*' of Sark to the Russian front had been furious that the doctor had certified him as fit to go, and had murdered him for it.

4

THE MODEL OCCUPATION

The behaviour of the local leaders of the Channel Islands, particularly in Guernsey and Jersey, remains controversial to this day. At the time, they believed themselves to have had no choice, and did the best they could under difficult circumstances. Abandoned by London and told to make do, they genuinely thought that resistance to the Germans was impossible. Their job was to manage the occupation for the Germans and to minimise the suffering of their populations. But by the time the war had ended, they had become the objects of severe criticism and one wrote that he wasn't sure if he'd be knighted – or hanged.

British military officers sent to the islands after the war were critical of the behaviour of many islanders who co-operated quite closely with the Germans. There were examples of islanders, including political leaders, crossing the line. These included public references to British troops as 'the enemy', offering substantial monetary rewards for informers when there was a wave of pro-Allied graffiti on the islands, and most significantly, turning over to the Germans the few remaining Jews on the islands, who would eventually die in Auschwitz.

The behaviour of the local population on Sark, and in particular that of the Dame, Mrs Hathaway, should be seen in that context. Mrs Hathaway was proud of the way she handled her many German visitors, all of whom signed her guest book.

They would often add expressions of appreciation for her hospitality, writing such things as 'always delighted with a nice reception'. She even encouraged the teaching of German to the island's children. Twenty-two of them took part in German lessons held not at the school but in her home, the Seigneurie. Just before the commando raid in October 1942, those lessons became compulsory.

She was also proud of her small acts of defiance. For example, as she later wrote, she:

> Made a point of putting banned anti-Fascist books such as *Sawdust Caesar* and *The House that Hitler Built* in a prominent place on my sitting room bookshelf where they were bound to be seen. It was fun to watch the Germans eyeing them, but I was never asked to move them, which was disappointing because I had planned to say, 'Take them away by all means. Everybody on the island has already read them in any case.'[1]

She relished the petty acts of defiance of the island's fishermen, who were forced to take German soldiers on board to ensure they didn't attempt to flee to England in their boats. The fisherman, she wrote, 'amused themselves by deliberately steering the boats into large waves, watching the German guards getting well-soaked and often sea-sick'.[2] And she also took pleasure in gently teasing the Germans: 'We never disagreed with the Germans openly, but we could annoy by asking ostensibly silly questions, such as "Haven't you landed in England yet?" or "I suppose Russia has by now been conquered."'[3]

But when she had her first opportunity to actually challenge the Germans and support the Allied war effort, she didn't rise to the occasion. As she told the story in her memoir, a few days after the Germans arrived, three young men, two French and one Polish, arrived in a small dinghy on Sark. They were brought to the Seigneurie and begged her help to get to England, where they were keen to join the fight against the Germans. She told them she could not help them, and that it was practically impossible to reach England in their small boat. She advised them to give themselves up, which they presumably did.

She later had another opportunity to help British soldiers who had been landed on Guernsey by submarine and wound up hiding in the empty home of her daughter on that island. She went over to Guernsey, met the men, and explained to them, as she had to the French and Polish young men, that she could not aid them in their escape. In the end, they too were advised to surrender to the Germans.

She strongly believed that there was no choice. 'We could do no good by sabotage,' she later wrote. 'There could be no underground movement where there was absolutely no contact with the outside world – we were like prisoners in a gaol with a garden to it.'[4] After the war, when challenged on this issue, Mrs Hathaway said she was not in the least ashamed of her behaviour. There was nothing to be gained, she said, by openly opposing the Germans 'or being rude to them'.[5]

Initially, the German soldiers made a positive impression on the islanders. As one local Channel Islands historian put it, 'The German army units in the Channel Islands in 1940 were crack infantry regiments, specially picked by the High Command to make a good impression on the British. Drunkenness, rowdyism, bullying and rape were unknown at this time'.[6] One Mrs Alsopp is quoted as saying of the Germans, 'Towards children and animals they were very kind'.[7]

'We found out later,' wrote the Dame of Sark:

> … that the first troops sent to occupy the Island were specially picked to impress on the British people that the Germans were well-behaved, well-disciplined and withal kind-hearted. The behaviour and discipline of these troops was excellent and it was rare to see a drunken soldier in those early days.[8]

It turns out, however, they were not hand-picked, and their good behaviour did not last long. There were plenty of examples of unsoldierly behaviour later in the war. At the time of the British commando raid in October 1942, one explanation offered for the slow German response to the sound of gunfire was that they may have thought the noise was drunken soldiers celebrating something.

Over time, the islanders grew less and less fond of the Germans. As the occupation continued, the quality of the Germans declined, according to the Dame. She looked down her nose at the petty bureaucrats she now faced who replaced the aristocratic and cultured officers she met on the very first day. She remembered:

> Instead of one sergeant and ten men, we were now bedevilled by swarms of officials who arrived and demanded statistics of every conceivable kind. These men had no military bearing. In spite of the uniforms they wore, they were nothing more than jumped-up peace-time clerks and office workers.[9]

She hated to have to comply with their constant demands regarding the island's finances, and their meddling in things they knew nothing about, such as which crops to plant. Similar complaints were made about the German bureaucrats on the other Channel Islands who were keen to introduce German ideas about efficiency, especially in farming, to the somewhat laid-back islanders.

Sark resident Julia Tremayne wrote about the Germans in her secret letters, published long after the war. She didn't see them as Aryan supermen, commenting that 'the officers here still strut around too fat to move, some of them. It is a wonder their horses don't give way under their weight.'[10] Tremayne was born in England, but came to live in Sark in her forties. Her secret letters were to her daughter, Betty, who spent the war in England, while Julia lived on Sark with her elder daughter,

Norah. She hid the letters in her home in Grand Dixcart, not only from the Germans but also from Norah. The Germans would almost certainly have punished her if the letters had been found.

Whatever the locals thought of the German soldiers, they didn't blame them for the deportations and other problems to come. A typical view was expressed by Channel Islands historian Roy McLoughlin, who wrote that, 'The Germans who gave their countrymen a bad reputation were those in the S.S. – the Schutzstaffel, Hitler's elite corps … In contrast, the German Army had a tradition and a code of honour. It disliked the methods of the S.S.'[11]

This attitude was embraced by the Germans themselves in the years after the war and became known as the 'myth of the unblemished Wehrmacht'. For the Germans, the myth suffered a fatal wounding in the 1990s when an exhibition toured German cities entitled 'War of Annihilation – Crimes of the Wehrmacht, 1941–1944'. But even today, the idea of a 'bad SS' and 'good Wehrmacht' survive in popular culture in Germany, as seen in the 2013 television series *Unsere Mütter, Unsere Väter* (shown in English-speaking countries as *Generation War*) for example. That series shows Germany Army soldiers shocked at the behaviour of the SS, and even attempting to stop some of the atrocities. Neither the SS nor the Gestapo ever put in an appearance on Sark, and yet the poisonous Nazi ideology of anti-Semitism with its 'Final Solution of the Jewish question' soon made itself felt.

It did not take long for the locals on Sark to discover just how unpleasant the German occupiers could be. In October 1940, barely three months into the occupation, the Germans decided to retaliate following the capture of two British soldiers on Guernsey. Fearful that there may be other British military personnel on the islands, everyone was obligated to register their personal details and to indicate if they had any relatives serving in the British forces. Identity cards were issued and all radios were confiscated. Meanwhile Sark's lighthouse, which had been abandoned by the British in June, was reoccupied by a small detachment from the Kriegsmarine.

Sark's tourist season was somewhat revived in the summers of 1940 and 1941, as local people from Guernsey came over to the island for a break. While the food situation in Guernsey was already becoming difficult, in Sark there was full-cream milk, locally made butter, fresh fish, crab and lobster in plentiful supply. As a result, the Dixcart Hotel, under the management of Misses Duckett and Page, remained open and some residents of the island took guests into their homes.

THE FINAL SOLUTION ON SARK

Annie Wranowsky was 46 years old at the time the Germans arrived on Sark. A divorcee, she had lived in the islands since 1934. She worked as a housekeeper and companion to a retired jeweller, Ernold Mason.[1] In the weeks before the German occupation began, Annie was taken to Guernsey where she was interned for some time as a German national. She returned to Sark just before the Germans arrived, in June 1940.

A few weeks after the Germans occupied the Channel Islands, orders were issued in Guernsey and Jersey regarding the registration of the Jews. Any Jews in Sark were required to register at the office of the seneschal. Historian David Fraser writes:

> We know from the available files on Guernsey that the Greffier [the government's clerk], under instructions from the Bailiff, forwarded the various Orders concerning Jews to the Seneschal of Sark, and that all the Orders relating to measures against the Jews were registered as a matter of routine in the Sark Greffe. Bailiff Carey at one point even informed Dr Brosch that there was a delay in getting complete information about the registration of Jews there because of the difficulties caused by the weather in maintaining communications between the Islands.[2]

Four months after the Germans began their 'model occupation', a Guernsey police inspector reported to A.J. Sherwill, a leader of the island government on Guernsey, about Annie Wranowsky, who was believed to be a German national. He wrote:

> Enquiries have been made by the Seneschal of Sark concerning the above named woman. She states that neither her parents nor grandparents were Jews and that she can trace back five generations in her family without encountering Jewish blood. Her passport, No. 558, issued in London on 13/2/39, is stamped with a 'J'.[3]

According to Fraser:

> The letters sent by [Island Police Inspector W.R.] Sculpher and Carey to the *Feldkommandantur* clearly establish that the Seneschal made active inquiries and interviewed Wranowsky about her Jewish status. There is no indication on the available documents that any form of objection about the morality or appropriateness of such measures or inquiries was raised by him. Moreover, there is absolutely no evidence that either the Seigneur or Dame of Sark ever questioned the measures. There can be no doubt, given the small size of the Island, the intimate nature of the involvement of the feudal rulers in all aspects of government and Island life more generally, and the close contacts which they had with German officials, that they were aware of the measures and of Wranowsky's situation.[4]

As it turned out, the Dame of Sark knew Annie Wranowsky quite well and was certainly aware of the threat hanging over her head. Despite Annie's protestations, just eighteen days later Inspector Sculpher wrote to the bailiff. The subject line of his message was 'Nationality of Jews'. It began, 'I have the honour to report that the Jews resident in the Bailiwick of Guernsey are of the following nationalities', and named five Jews, the last of whom was: 'Czech – WRANOWSKY, Annie, Clos de Ville, Sark'.

In other words, despite Annie's denial, the authorities in Guernsey continued to list her as being Jewish and made sure the Germans knew. As far as the Germans were aware, there was one possible Jewish person on Sark, and though she denied being Jewish, this issue preoccupied both the German authorities and local governments for many months to come. Such was the pathological nature of German Nazi anti-Semitism that the presence of a single Jew, even a 46-year-old housekeeper, was seen as such a threat that it required serious attention.

The Island Police continued to investigate. In a letter dated 8 January 1941 with the subject line 'Aliens', and written to the President of States Controlling Committee, a police inspector wrote:

> In checking the list of Aliens it has occurred to me that those living on Sark have not been included, as only those Aliens living in this Island were asked for. There are only three persons of foreign nationality living in Sark, Wranowsky has been returned, but I do not think the German Authorities have been informed of the two Americans whose particulars are forwarded herewith.

The phrase 'it has occurred to me' is striking; this police officer was trying to be even more helpful to the Germans by adding 'aliens' living on Sark as well as those in Guernsey, and reminding them of Annie's existence. The additional 'aliens' he discovered were Max Baird and Albert Fehenbach, both men in their seventies. He did not name Robert Hathaway, also an American citizen, who served as the Seigneur of Sark, presumably because he was also a British subject. At the time, the US was neutral, so the only practical effect of submitting the information to the Germans would be to remind them that a Jewish woman, Annie Wranowsky, lived on Sark.

In a June 1942 report to the SS, Oberkriegsverwaltungsrat Dr Wilhelm Casper, the chief administrator of the German occupation government for the Channel Islands, reported on all the Jews he could find in Guernsey and Jersey, and no longer included Annie in the list.[5] But she was not yet in the clear.

After the commando raid in October that year, John Leale, president of the Controlling Committee in Guernsey, wrote to the Germans with a list of the Jews who had been identified, and in an attempt to pre-empt any further correspondence on the matter, added this postscript: 'Apart from the Police no other States department has any information concerning Jews.'

By now it seemed as if Annie was due to be deported to the Continent, where her fate would be sealed. But according to historian Frederick Cohen, her status remained undecided and 'the Feldkommandantur annotated her deportation order "German nationality, has Jewish passport and is presently trying to prove her Aryan origin"'.

Annie continued in her efforts and by the third week of April 1943 she was granted a travel permit to Guernsey, 'the purpose of which was stated "to prove her Aryan descent and to visit a dentist". It would appear Wranowsky's appeal to prove her Aryan status was successful.' Some believe that this was due to the intervention of Mrs Hathaway. But Cohen disagrees:

> There is however no documentary evidence to support this theory. However their friendship is confirmed by a letter sent by the Dame to Mr Pleul in Guernsey dated 6 October 1941 requesting help in obtain [sic] German books for the lessons being given to 22 Sark children by Wranowsky does however state 'My friend Frau Wranowsky, whom you know is giving the lessons'.

In other words, Frau Wranowsky was the Dame's friend, but Mrs Hathaway was not going to raise any protest at the possibility of her deportation with the other Jewish women found in Guernsey. The Dame was perfectly capable of expressing her anger at the Germans and demanding that they change their behaviour when she felt they had crossed a line. This occurred notably when she was given an order banning fraternisation between German soldiers and local women on the island. The order was given in the wake of the spread of venereal disease among the German forces. Fraser wrote:

> A notice concerning venereal disease was not just an insult to a lady, but its implication that Sarkee women were consorting with Germans was too much for the moral sensibilities of the Dame. There is no available evidence, on the other hand, at all that the Dame of Sark found reason to offer any formal objections to the anti-Jewish Orders registered on Sark. Legalised anti-Semitism was apparently perfectly acceptable.[6]

Whatever the reason, Annie's success in proving her Aryan status – or as she put it, 'five generations in her family without encountering Jewish blood' – undoubtedly saved her life. The Jewish women in Guernsey who were not able to do so died in Auschwitz.

The search for Jews on Sark and elsewhere in the Channel Islands continued for years to come. Two weeks after the British commando raid in October 1942, Dr Casper wrote on behalf of the *Feldkommandantur* to the Bailiff of Jersey and the president of the Controlling Committee of the states of Guernsey saying, 'I request you to let me know full and accurate personal information regarding Jews who left the islands during the month of June, 1940. The information should include the exact last address of these Jews.'

Dr Casper was now keen to know about Jews who had fled *before* the Germans arrived. One wonders why; possibly the Germans were looking to confiscate their property. His request was passed on by the Controlling Committee to the Island Police. An official there replied, 'I beg to inform you that prior to the occupation Police have no record of Jews resident in Guernsey.'

THE RAIDERS

The Small Scale Raiding Force (SSRF), also known as No. 62 Commando, had already established a fierce reputation before they ever set foot on Sark. The SSRF was a part of the Special Forces under the command of Combined Operations, led from October 1941 by Lord Louis Mountbatten. But it also had special ties to the very secretive Special Operations Executive (SOE), headed by Major General Sir Colin McVean Gubbins – better known by his code name, 'M'. (He chose this because it was the initial of his middle name.) SOE was set up in July 1940, following the withdrawal from Dunkirk, and engaged in covert operations behind German lines throughout the war. It was based in London at 64 Baker Street, under the name 'Inter Services Research Bureau'. Many of its exploits remained secret for decades after the war ended.

Like all such commando formations, the SSRF consisted of volunteers, men who were hand-picked by their commanders. Highly motivated and extremely well trained, their exploits soon became legend. The SSRF's founders, Major Gus March-Phillips and Captain Geoffrey Appleyard, met in a foxhole on the beach in Dunkirk and quickly became friends. The SSRF was their idea and was gradually built up to a unit of around forty officers and men, based from March 1942 in Anderson Manor, near Poole in Dorset.

Anderson Manor, which was code-named Station 62, is a 400-year-old manor house with elaborate gardens and it was here that the commandos lived and trained. They used the walled garden for pistol and tommy-gun practice and to this day you can find spent cartridges lodged in the mud. To the north of the manor there was a grenade range in a pit. Among the trees on the drive, across from the River Winterborne which runs alongside the manor, was an assault course. In addition to training at Anderson, the commandos learned rock climbing in the Lake District and swimming in the sea down at Poole. These skills were to come in useful during the raid on Sark later that year.

There are only a few traces left today of the commandos' stay in Anderson Manor. There was a cherub that used to adorn a fountain in the front courtyard. It became an obvious target for pistols, crossbows and other weapons and all that remains is the head, now incorporated in the garden walls. Inside the home, it is said that you can still see knife marks in the walls left by the commandos. There is a small chapel next to the house where some of the men would pray before going on a raid, and a brass plaque was placed there in 1988 during a special service honouring their memory. Other than that, the house and garden are largely unchanged since March-Phillips and Appleyard came there in early 1942.

Among the British officers involved with setting up the SSRF and liaising with them were Ian Fleming. Fleming may have based the James Bond character on a composite of the men he worked with, including March-Phillips, Appleyard and the legendary Danish commando Anders Lassen.

Their first mission in January 1942, code-named Operation Postmaster, was an audacious raid in West Africa, carried out on board a sailing ship known as *Maid Honor*, which resulted in the successful seizure of both a German and Italian ship in the port of Fernando Po. Key figures in the later raid on Sark, including Lassen and Appleyard, were involved in this first raid.

This successful carrying out of a high-risk mission impressed Churchill and other successful raids followed.

It was not until 14 August 1942 that the men of the SSRF got a chance to go into action in Europe. Their first mission was Operation Barricade, a reconnaissance raid on the French coast. They landed ¾ mile north of where they needed to be, and came upon a German patrol. In the firefight that followed, March-Phillips estimated that they killed between three and six of the enemy, wounding three or four more. The men of the SSRF suffered no casualties. Though they did not succeed in taking any prisoners, the raid proved the effectiveness of a small raiding force.

On 2 September 1942, the SSRF were given the target of the German-held Casquets Lighthouse in the Channel Islands, near Alderney. It was their first operation in the German-occupied Channel Islands. The raid, code-named Operation Dryad, was a complete triumph. The commandos made the journey on the high-speed Motor Torpedo Boat (MTB) 344, known as the 'Little Pisser', commanded by Lieutenant Freddie Bourne and with a crew of eight men, as was their habit.

Bourne would silence the engines as they approached their target and the commandos would get into the small wooden and canvas Goatley and paddle towards shore. A Goatley was built to carry ten men, though the commandos would test that limit as they approached the Casquets Lighthouse. The Goatley weighed about 150kg and could be assembled by two men in two minutes. Fred Goatley had designed the boat that bore his name and it proved hugely successful. By the end of the war, the War Office had ordered 1,000 of them to be built.

After reaching the shore, the commandos scrambled up a cliff to their target. That night, they surprised the Germans and took the entire garrison of seven men without firing a shot. In addition to capturing live prisoners, among them professional telegraphers, they got hold of codebooks, radio logs and other valuable information.

MTB 344 was a 60ft long vessel with a small bridge. There was room enough for its crew to rest, but nowhere to actually sleep. The two 18in torpedo tubes had been removed to make room for commando operations. And things were added too, such as something to allow a little boat to hang from the hull. The boat was built by Thornycroft for the navy, but the army soon took her over for covert operations.

Motor torpedo boats were high-speed craft of a type known to many navies at that time. In the United States, they were known as Patrol Torpedo (PT) boats and one (PT-109) was famously commanded by John F. Kennedy, the future president. A British MTB was lightly armed, and as such was no match for the German *schnellboot*, which patrolled the English Channel. Usually they carried torpedoes, and sometimes depth charges, but in the case of MTB 344 these had been removed to make room for men and equipment, including the wood and canvas landing boats known as 'Goatleys'.

Boats like Bourne's MTB 344 could move quite quickly, but the trade-off was that they were quite noisy. As they approached their destinations, where silence was essential, they relied on auxiliary motors that were nearly silent. The key thing about them was their speed; they were good for the fast getaway, but not so effective if actually called upon to fight.

As author Angus Konstam explained:

> MTB commanders were playing a dangerous game, fighting at night, at point-blank range and in boats that were little more than high-speed mahogany and plywood fuel tanks. In a private war where a clip of 20mm shells or a single heavy gun round could virtually destroy an MTB, to loiter in the battle area after the torpedoes were fired was tantamount to suicide.

In other words, asking Freddie Bourne to linger around Sark for a few hours while the commandos landed and carried out their mission was no small matter.

Over the course of the war, Bourne commanded MTB 344 seventeen times. As he put it in an interview many years later, 'She was an exciting boat and I enjoyed her very much.'

A number of those who participated in Operation Dryad would be called upon just a few weeks later to take part in the raid on Sark, including Appleyard and Lieutenant Patrick Laurence Dudgeon, and much about the raid anticipated what they would try on Sark. As they left in their Goatley on their way back to the waiting MTB, Appleyard slipped on the rocks and broke a bone in his ankle. As Freddie Bourne later remembered, the Germans captured at the Casquets Lighthouse were 'elderly chaps', probably reservists. One or two of the Germans who were awakened from deep slumber by the commandos wore hairnets. 'It was somewhat effeminate,' recalled Bourne, who thought at first that they might have been women.[2]

Five days later, the SSRF went again to the Channel Islands, this time in a reconnaissance mission code-named Operation Branford. Their target was the tiny island of Burhou, just north of Alderney. It was a successful raid, gathering intelligence and remaining undetected by the Germans.

After a string of successes, and no casualties inflicted by the enemy for some time, the next SSRF raid, just days later, had tragic results. In Operation Aquatint on 12–13 September, the commandos were given the target of German defensive positions on the French coast, in the Calvados region. March-Phillips pulled together a small team of men and though Appleyard came along on the ship, he did not land because of his ankle injury. As he waited on board MTB 344, which had taken the men over from England, disaster unfolded before his eyes. March-Phillips and his men quickly came upon German soldiers and a firefight ensued. In the course of the short battle that followed, several of the SSRF men, including March-Phillips, were killed. Others were captured. None of the eleven men who landed that night returned as planned to Anderson Manor. Appleyard stood on board the boat helpless to do anything.

It was in the aftermath of the disaster that was Aquatint that the decision was made to launch the raid on Sark. Appleyard was now in command of the SSRF. Without their inspiring leader March-Phillips, men like Appleyard and Lassen who had been with him from the beginning were angry and bent on revenge. Appleyard put together a team of men for the next raid, code-named Operation Basalt. The men selected were among the best trained, most highly motivated and deadliest group of soldiers ever assembled.

Major John Geoffrey Appleyard was 25 years old and one of the youngest majors in the British Army. Known to his men as 'Apple', he was born to a middle-class family in Leeds. Appleyard studied at Cambridge, and was an expert rower and skier, winning an important Anglo-Norwegian competition. In his letters home, he often wrote about his fellow skiers, including Germans he met in pre-war competitions.

He had another passion as well: birds. Appleyard's father remembered one incident from long before the war. He wrote:

> On one ornithological expedition, Geoff persuaded the gatherer of the gulls' eggs on the Bempton Cliffs, near Flamborough, to permit him to take his place on the loop of rope and be lowered over the edge, where he swung himself to and fro, hundreds of feet above the sea, until able to make contact with the side of the overhanging cliff and gather the coveted trophy as a proof of success.[3]

This kind of thing would come in handy as he climbed the cliffs of Casquets Lighthouse, and later, Sark.

After completing university, Appleyard began working for his father's automobile repair business in Leeds. With war clouds threatening Europe, he joined the army reserves, and was mobilised with the outbreak of fighting in September 1939. Appleyard proved to be a somewhat unconventional officer. While working with his men, he once stripped down to the waist and dug trenches with them to boost their flagging morale, was caught out, and was reprimanded for conduct unbecoming an officer. This attitude served him well in the commandos.

With the outbreak of war, he expressed very strong views about the Nazi regime. He wrote: 'Funny how relative everything is – you don't really appreciate a holiday till it's over. The same way you don't really appreciate your liberty until it's threatened. But I'll never be made to say "Heil Hitler". I'd sooner die.'[4]

While serving in France, he was concerned, rightly it turned out, that there may be some in the British Government who would be willing to surrender to the Germans or reach an accommodation with them. He wanted nothing to do with this. As France was falling to the advancing Wehrmacht, he wrote to his family: 'Anyway, above all things, I do hope that we don't make any kind of treaty – even though France does pack up. We would never be able to hold our heads up again.'[5]

Appleyard was delighted to be accepted into the commandos in the autumn of 1940. He described their role to his family as, 'a mobile fighting unit that can get anywhere in the shortest possible time to do a job'.[6] He was convinced that he was accepted because of his experience skiing and rowing – and thrilled to be working with his close friend Gus March-Phillips. He described what he'd need to do as an officer in charge of commandos. He told his family:

> I shall be in command of 23 picked men – all volunteers …
> Everything depends on the men we choose … This thing can either be a flop or a colossal success, and so much depends on the men – they must be utterly reliable, steady and intelligent … I can know every man personally, the sort of job he can do, his good points and his weak ones.[7]

It appears that in one letter to him, his parents said they were praying for him. 'Don't pray for my safety or for my speedy return,' he told them, 'but pray that I am alive to my responsibilities, courageous in danger, and that I have the strength to do my bit of job to the utmost.'[8]

One of the men Appleyard chose was Captain Colin Ogden-Smith, 32 years old and married with one child, who had already had his share of commando adventures before joining the SSRF. Ogden-Smith was one of the few commandos who escaped from the Greek island of Crete as it was falling into German hands. Though he was recommended for a decoration by Appleyard for his role in the Sark raid, Ogden-Smith was reprimanded a few weeks later for an article that appeared in the London *Evening Standard*. Apparently, his father gave the press some details of an operation, possibly Operation Basalt. His army records show a recommendation that he not be used on the highly secret SOE operations 'but only on "straight" Commando stuff'.[9]

Second Lieutenant Anders Frederik Lassen was probably the most colourful character in a unit full of colourful characters. He was tall and slim, with very pale blue eyes. Born to a wealthy Danish family, he was just 22 years old at the time of the Sark raid. Lassen, known as 'Andy' to his fellow commandos, was a skilled hunter, especially effective with knife, bow and gun. A deeply patriotic man, he was furious at the Germans for invading and occupying his country in 1940, and he quickly made his way to England where he joined up with the SOE.

Despite having had no formal army training, Lassen's talents were quickly recognised and he rose from private to lieutenant. It was said of him that, unlike Englishmen, he had no problem killing another man from up close, with a knife. Though already recognised as an expert in silent killing, prior to the Sark raid he'd never actually used his knife in combat. Lassen was an enthusiastic advocate of the use of the bow and arrow in combat and wrote a memorandum to his superior officers recommending its adoption by the commandos. One former commando claims that upon his arrival at Anderson Manor, he was sent upstairs to the room he'd share with the Dane. When he opened the door, Lassen was pointing a crossbow at it – and fired. The arrow came dangerously close to his head.

David Smee, a fellow commando officer who shared a room with Lassen, recalled:

> He kept me awake most of the night, cleaning his pistol and sharpening his fighting knife while talking to himself about 'Killing the fuckers!' Nobody else could have put such venom into knife and pistol cleaning. It was in keeping with his enormously forceful nature. I was glad not to be his enemy.[10]

Following the devastating results of Operation Aquatint, and especially the loss of Gus March-Phillips, a number of men from E Troop of No. 12 Commando (also known as the 'Irish Commando' because they had been based in Northern Ireland) were attached to the SSRF before the Sark raid. Though they were battle-hardened veterans themselves, some of them having taken part in the March 1942 St Nazaire raid, the newcomers were given specialised night-time training to bring them up to speed with the SSRF.

Their commander was Captain Philip Hugh Pinckney, known as 'PHP' to his men. Pinckney was educated at Eton and then Cambridge. Like Appleyard, he enlisted in the Territorial Army before the outbreak of the war. After serving some time in the artillery, he volunteered for the commandos in 1940. He led his men in raids on the French coast and in Norway in 1941, and the following year planned a daring raid to steal a German Focke-Wulf Fw 190 fighter aircraft from a Luftwaffe airfield near the French coast. The plan was abandoned after a Luftwaffe pilot inadvertently landed an aircraft of this type at an RAF base in Wales, making the commando raid unnecessary.

According to Horace Stokes, who came with Pinckney and the men of No. 12 Commando to join up with the SSRF, Pinckney took the commando style of no division between officers and men:

… to another level as he was not one for bullshit; he allowed us to wear what we needed to wear according to what it was we were doing. This was of course completely at odds with how the 'normal' army operated and sometimes it didn't win friends with senior officers. However, because of things like this, we began to earn a bit of a reputation for being one of the toughest and most effective sections in the Commando.[11]

Lieutenant Patrick Laurence Dudgeon was 22 years old and had been born in Cairo. A tall man, he was nicknamed 'Toomai' after the elephant boy in a Rudyard Kipling story. In one of his military files he rated himself as fluent in speaking, reading and writing German, though apparently with a Swiss accent. Despite that, his German came in handy on the Sark raid, for afterwards he was awarded a Military Cross by Lord Louis Mountbatten, the chief of Combined Operations, stating that he proved to be 'invaluable as an interpreter'.[12]

Second Lieutenant Graham Salter Young, born in 1900, was the oldest man picked to participate in the raid on Sark. He was recruited to the SSRF by March-Phillips as soon as it was formed and was described in an official report as 'one of the best small boat men in the country'.[13] Young had served during the First World War and had been a commando posted to Egypt and Crete in the early days of the Second World War. He received his commission as an officer just five months before the Sark raid.

Quite a bit is known about the six officers who participated in the raid, but much less about the 'Other Ranks', as they are known. Private Bruce Ogden-Smith was the exception. He was Colin's younger brother, recruited by him to the SSRF. Lord Ashcroft writes that he:

… could easily have become an officer. When people asked him why he had not opted for officer training (and the prestige and comforts that went with it), he explained that he was quite happy as a sergeant. In fact, he had once given in to temptation and started an officers' training course, but this ended abruptly when he wrote rude words on an intelligence test that he thought was a waste of time.

Corporal James Edgar participated in Operation Branford, the last SSRF raid before the disaster of Aquatint, and was on the Sark raid. So was Corporal Flint.

It is generally agreed that twelve commandos participated in Operation Basalt, seven of them from the original SSRF and five from No. 12 Commando. It is known with certainty who nine of them were – Appleyard, Lassen, Pinckney, Dudgeon, Young, the Ogden-Smith brothers and corporals Edgar and Flint.[14] These were the men who were about to go to the heavily fortified island of Sark with the aim of capturing at least one of the 300 German soldiers based there.

7

DEPORTATIONS

Only a few days before the commando raid in October 1942, the people of Sark and the other Channel Islands were getting a taste of just how badly the 'model occupation' was turning out. The story of the deportations of civilians from the Channel Islands to Germany began thousands of kilometres away, and a year earlier, in Iran. In September 1941, British and Soviet troops occupied that country, which had been neutral, and the British took the decision to remove from the country hundreds of Germans who fell into their hands. As Tom Remfrey tells the story, 'Women and children and elderly men were forcibly repatriated to Germany through the adjoining border of neutral Turkey. Their male relatives, husbands and men of military age were subsequently deported to Australia.'[1]

On 20 October 1941, a furious Hitler gave the order to retaliate by deporting the only British subjects he could reach, the Channel Islanders. He wrote: 'Orders will follow with regard to the deportation to the mainland of English inhabitants who do not form part of the native population of the islands.'[2] The distinction between 'the native population of the islands' and 'English inhabitants' was an important one for the Nazis. They had already decided that after the war, which would end in a German victory, the islands would not be returned to British rule and would probably become French. They would be used as a holiday resort for the 'Strength through Joy' organisation.

For a year nothing was done about the Führer's order and the islanders were spared. But when an angry Hitler learned that his orders had not been carried out, he demanded action. Over the course of two days, on 16 and 18 September 1942, nearly 2,000 Channel Islanders, men, women and children, were deported to internment camps in Germany. The order to deport them had come directly from the Führer's headquarters. Some of those deported were given as little as twelve hours' notice. Their only crime had been that they were considered to be English rather than local islanders. No one in London knew about the deportations which, together with the atrocities on Alderney, constituted the most significant German war crime carried out on British soil.

In Sark, the Germans served eleven residents of the island with orders to report for deportation to Germany. Among them was 63-year-old Major H.J. Skelton and his wife, Madge. The Dame of Sark, who had done so little to help her 'friend' Annie Wranowsky who faced the risk of being sent to death camps, intervened to get Major Skelton exempted. She sent a handwritten note to R.O. Falla, the agricultural officer in Guernsey, trying to get two men released from the deportations. One of them was Skelton, who served as the island's agricultural officer. 'As regards Skelton,' she wrote, 'the work will fall on me in the end and I'll have to get you to come over soon and help me straighten out all the tangles.' But to no avail. Falla replied that they'd obtained an exemption for the other man, Bishop. 'I also had a good try to get Skelton off,' he wrote, 'but they were adamant.'[3] Why the Germans were adamant about deporting a retired major will soon become clear.

The day came for all the Sark deportees to report, but only nine of the eleven turned up. The two missing were the Skeltons. When it became clear that the Skeltons weren't coming, the Germans searched every house on the island, and at dawn the following day Mrs Hathaway was summoned. 'Major S— was dead,' she wrote, 'and his wife was in a ghastly state, having stabbed herself in sixteen places.'[4] The major was found dead on the common at La Rondellerie. The badly injured Mrs Skelton was rushed off to Guernsey for medical care, and eventually returned to Sark. Her suicide attempt got her removed from the list of deportees and she spent the war years in Sark.

The Germans learned that the major had left a message with the Dame. She was interrogated but revealed nothing. She insisted that the only message she'd received was an oral one, as they'd handed over some jewellery for safe-keeping. The Dame was not being completely honest with her German 'guests' on this occasion. As she wrote in her memoir, 'The day before they were due to leave they called at our house for a few moments and asked me to take charge of three letters and some jewellery which, they explained in a perfectly normal way, they did not wish to leave in an empty house.'[5] They were in 'a tragic state of panic', she explained. But apparently they did not warn the Dame of their intention to take their own lives. She took their letters and hid them in the straw of her rabbit hutches. The Germans never found them, but neither have archivists. The only message surviving from Major Skelton to the Dame was written two years earlier, praising her effusively for her leadership during the difficult time of German occupation.[6]

On the day of Major Skelton's funeral, 29 September, the Dame wrote in German to Oberleutnant Herdt thanking him for his 'understanding and kindness with which you and the Doctor have come to assist Mrs. Skelton'. She added that, 'May both of you be assured that we … firmly believe, also the inhabitants of the island, will always keep both of you in grateful memory.'

Some people in the Channel Islands believe that there was more to Major Skelton than appeared on the surface. Noting that he chose to move permanently to Sark in June 1940 on the very eve of the German occupation (though he'd owned a home there for several years) it is considered a possibility that he was 'embedded' in Sark by British Military Intelligence.[7] Who else would choose to come over to from England to Sark to live under German occupation when nearly all the traffic was in the other direction? Richard Le Tissier adds that 'it seems rather strange that an experienced Army officer, fluent in German, was not offered at least a desk job at that stage of the war, even at retirement age.'[8] Another explanation given for Skelton's 'panic' on hearing he was to be deported to Germany was that he had suffered there as a prisoner of war during the First World War and couldn't bear to face imprisonment yet again.[9]

One historian who has gone on record with his suspicions about the major is William M. Bell, who writes:

The Germans had become noticeably suspicious of John Skelton, a German linguist, who had served as Major in the Royal Engineers. They considered him to be a security risk and suspected that he might be a British agent. The Major was very wary about letting the Germans know too much about his past, including his involvement in the Spanish Civil War. Whilst he never publicly acknowledged it, he was believed to be a Jew and feared the consequences of falling into German hands.[10]

John Nettles writes that Skelton 'was also a Jew and it is thought that it was this, above all else, that caused him to take his own life'.[11]

The *Inselkommandant* (island commandant), Oberleutnant Herdt, wrote a report on Skelton and sent it to his commanders in Guernsey on 21 September 1942. He noted that Skelton had arrived on Sark 'the day that St Peter Port harbour was bombed', and added the following:

Mr Skelton, a former major in the Royal Engineers, is known to be anti-German by Sark people. As an officer of engineers he has sufficient military knowledge about the defence's deployment and measures to observe and assess them. When the minefields were being laid during his time on Sark, Major Skelton approached the sappers with the suggestion that they should tell him where the mines were, as he, Major Skelton, should know since it concerned his piece of land and it would have to be cleared once the war was over. Apart from this, he had to be able to enter the minefield in order to oil his wind-pump. I consider his evacuation necessary on counter-intelligence grounds alone.[12]

Whether he was simply spooked by the possibility of another internment in Germany or had other secrets to hide, the death of Major Skelton was a tragedy and illustrated how even under the conditions of a 'model occupation' the Germans brought suffering to local residents. A year after his death, his widow Madge invited *Inselkommandant* Herdt and his doctor for coffee at her home. The letter, which survives in the archives, is written in fluent German, and apparently the German officers accepted the invitation.

Though the 'myth of the unblemished Wehrmacht' had taken root, and would persist for decades after the war, orders now coming from Berlin were causing some unease among the islanders. The most important of these was the order to deport eleven Sarkees to internment camps in Germany. That was a clear breach of the Germans' commitment to letting the islanders continue to run their own affairs if they promised not to resist the occupation.

The islanders had settled into life under German rule, with its curfew and restrictions on fishermen, its minefields and its barbed wire, and its German language classes for the children. Roy McLoughlin writes:

Shortages of clothes beset the Islanders as in Jersey and Guernsey but, in a small community, Sarkees could more easily make exchanges and, in a general way, support each other. Sibyl Hathaway turned one of her rooms at the Seigneurie into a workshop where jackets and other garments were made out of curtains and any other material brought in.[13]

The Dame wrote:

All our thoughts and conversations became focussed on food. We had masses of lobsters, but had no means to vary the way of cooking them, and the same was true of rabbits. When lobster is the main dish day after day, month in month out, let me assure you that you become heartily sick of the sight of it.[14]

For some, like Annie Wranowsky, there was the ever-present threat of deportation to something far worse than an internment camp, even if the full horrors of the Holocaust were not yet widely known. But for the German soldiers based on Sark, it remained a 'kleine Paradies', the murder of their doctor having been the only act of violence on the island in the first two years of the occupation.

All that was to change on the night of 3–4 October 1942.

8

APPLEYARD TAKES COMMAND

Following the disaster of Operation Aquatint and the death of Gus March-Phillips, Combined Operations Headquarters decided not to attempt the French coast again, but rather to return the SSRF to the Channel Islands for their next raid. These raids had several objectives, the principal of which was to capture one or more German prisoners. A German prisoner who was knowledgeable and who gave up information under questioning by MI19, the section of Military Intelligence responsible for prisoner interrogation, was worth his weight in gold.

It must be remembered that there were limits to what British and other Allied military commanders could learn about the state of German defences from aerial reconnaissance and other intelligence gathering methods at the time. Talking with a German soldier who had experience on the ground was invaluable. It was highly unlikely that any of them would be voluntarily coming over to England any time soon, which is why it was deemed necessary to capture some of them, and bring them over by force.

It may be hard to imagine today how little was actually known in London about life on the Channel Islands in 1942. The islands were completely cut off. All wireless sets had been confiscated (though some remained hidden, including one held by the Dame of Sark). The only letters allowed out or in were the rare and very short Red Cross messages, which were heavily censored. These sometimes took months to reach their destinations. Fishermen on the islands were severely restricted in how far they could take their boats out for fear they would sail off to England, as some had done in the very early days of the occupation.

Attempts early in the war to land British commandos on some of the Channel Islands to leave them there to gather intelligence had failed. And despite rumours that there had been an SOE operative based on Sark, or the suspicions that the unfortunate Major Skelton may have worked for British Intelligence, in reality the islands had 'gone dark'. Even the large-scale deportations of 2,000 islanders in September 1942 had gone unnoticed in Britain.

In short, the Allied commanders in London were twenty months away from the D-Day landings in Normandy without enough hard intelligence about the state of Hitler's Atlantic Wall defences, not only in France, but even in the small part of Britain the German forces occupied. The capture of a live prisoner was the main reason for carrying out the small-scale raids on the Channel Islands, even if that was not fully understood at the time by many, including the islanders themselves. This is made clear by something Julia Tremayne wrote in her secret wartime letters. Complaining about a later raid on the island, she wrote that she could not:

> … see myself what good the landing down here does. The last one was October 1942 and brought us nothing but misery … If it meant shortening the war we did not mind but all this is nerve-racking and I am afraid even my own shadow sometimes makes me jump.[1]

What Mrs Tremayne did not understand was that the raids were designed precisely to do just that – shorten the war – by ensuring that the Allies had the best possible intelligence on German defences in the territories they occupied.

Fortunately, the commandos themselves understood the reasoning behind the raids, and this was clearly expressed by one of the men who took part, Horace 'Stokey' Stokes. As he put it in his diary, 'The main purpose of the mission was to take prisoners and get them back to England for questioning about German defences along the French coast and the state of their equipment and morale.'[2] In weighing up whether the raid was a success or not, the principal test is whether a live German prisoner was taken, and what information he gave up.

Though capturing a prisoner was the main purpose of raids like Operation Basalt, it was not the only purpose. Other reasons for doing the 'butcher and bolt' raids included terrorising the enemy, compelling the Germans to waste men and resources beefing up defences in places of no strategic value, stirring up local resistance in territories they occupied, and finally, raising morale on the home front.

German propaganda at the time played up just how comfortable their soldiers were on the English Channel Islands. This was not entirely inaccurate, for Wehrmacht medical orderly Werner Rang and his friends considered Sark to be a 'kleine Paradies', while Baron von Aufsess wrote that Sark was 'the island of one's dreams'. It infuriated Churchill that German soldiers could feel so unthreatened on occupied British territory. It was time to turn 'the island of one's dreams' into a nightmare.

A good illustration of the 'butcher and bolt' strategy working very effectively was the aftermath of the commando raid on the Casquets Lighthouse, where the entire German garrison was taken without firing a shot. The garrison sent in to replace them was considerably larger.

By mid-1942, there were approximately 37,000 German troops tied down occupying the Channel Islands. This was a staggering waste of more than an entire infantry division loaded down with heavy weapons at a time when the German Army was fighting for its very survival in Russia. As Madeleine Bunting writes, this was 'a higher concentration of armed forces per square mile than in Germany itself. The islands' population after the evacuation was just over sixty thousand, so there was more than one German to every two islanders.'[3] In Sark, the ratio was even higher. Churchill is said to have called the German bases on the Channel Islands 'the biggest and cheapest prisoner-of-war camps behind Allied front lines'.[4]

Where the raids proved to be somewhat less successful was in stiffening resistance to German rule. Opinions differ as to how the locals reacted to commando raids. Looking back after many years, everyone welcomed the raids, delighted that Britain had not forgotten what Churchill would later call 'our dear Channel Islands'. But at the time, as Mrs Tremayne's letters and other documents show, rather than help to 'set Europe ablaze', commando raids made daily life worse for the victims of Nazi occupation, and turned some islanders against the British for doing so.

One final aim of raids such as Operation Basalt was to raise morale on the home front, though this was complicated by the fact that the raids needed to be kept secret. The October 1942 raid on Sark had a different character, due to the German decision to publicise their version of what happened. As a result, the British public learned for the first time of the daring raid, and the newspapers were full of accounts of what the commandos had done. And at a time when the British Army was recovering from the stinging defeat in France more than two years earlier, and the more recent disastrous raid on Dieppe, good news was most welcome. Raids like Basalt proved that the British Army was still standing, fighting and inflicting pain on the Germans.

By mid-September 1942, the SSRF, now under the command of Appleyard, began getting ready for the next in its series of raids. This one targeted Sark, and like the other raids had as its primary goal the capture of one or more German prisoners. Because of the disaster of Operation Aquatint, the SSRF could not carry out the raid on its own. There were seven officers and men from the SSRF ready to go. Five men from 'E' Troop of No. 12 Commando under the command of Captain Philip Hugh Pinckney joined them.[5]

It is not known today how Sark was picked as the target, but it is likely that Appleyard himself suggested it. SSRF officers had a say in choosing where they would go next, and Appleyard knew Sark quite well from pre-war visits he'd made with his family. All the Channel Islands, including Sark, were popular tourist destinations for British people in the 1930s. The well-off Appleyard family were regular visitors to the island, where Geoffrey and his siblings would explore the island's paths, beaches, caves and cliffs. Geoffrey's sister, Jenny, had only the fondest memories of Sark, 'where we spent long days exploring caves and rock pools, and swimming and diving in the astonishing sapphire depths of Venus Pool'.[6] Jenny Appleyard loved the Channel Islands so much that after the war, she and her husband moved permanently to Herm, the island that she could see from Sark.

A few weeks before the October 1942 raid, Appleyard wrote to his father mentioning that he'd seen the Sark light during a raid on another Channel Island. 'I should like to land on Sark again sometime,' he mused.[7] Weeks before the raid took place, Appleyard had a chance to visit his parents. As his father later recalled:

> We couldn't, at that time, understand why he was so keen to see a cinema film which we had taken on a family holiday in the Channel Islands some years before the war. But after the raid was announced in the papers, we realised that he had been refreshing his memory of one of the islands so that he could land with his men by night and lead them with sureness and certainty across the same beaches and up the same cliffs as he played upon as a boy.[8]

In addition to the Appleyard family home movies, the commandos would certainly have relied on guides to the island, none more important than *La Trobe's Guide to Sark*, which was first published in 1914. The guide encouraged visitors to swim in the bay and added that afterwards:

> After a fairly stiff climb the top of the curious headland, called the Hog's Back, is attained. From the sea the origin of the name can be better seen, and from there one can easily recognise the high curved back and the nozzle thrust out to sea.[9] [In maps prepared by the German occupiers years later, they renamed the Hog's Back '*Schweinsrücken*'.]

The *La Trobe Guide* added that 'a descent can be made with care at the point of the Hog's Back, the Point du Château, but care must be taken with the crumbling rocks'.[10] The inspiration for the decision to land the commandos at Pointe Château and climb to the top of the Hog's Back is clearly to be found in this guide, which is still available today. (The La Trobe family produced a 100th anniversary edition in 2014.)

In addition to personal memories, family home movies and a popular walking guide to the island, the commandos would also have had access to aerial reconnaissance photos. Unfortunately, these proved to be of rather poor quality, indicating, for example, the presence of a German machine-gun emplacement on top of the Hog's Back – which turned out to be something rather different. Later in the war, the Royal Air Force would become much better at this sort of thing, but in September 1942 the aerial photos at the disposal of the commandos were not particularly helpful.

Finally, it appears that some intelligence about Sark may have been collected from one of the prisoners captured at the previous raid on the Casquets Lighthouse. That man, the 21-year-old wireless operator Funkgefreiter Reineck, gave a very detailed, if not entirely accurate, account of the German garrison on Sark.[11]

In mid-September 1942, Appleyard summoned the commandos into his office where he had laid out on a table dozens of aerial photos of Sark. In addition to these, there was a model of the island.[12] One cannot overstate the importance of a physical model, for the route the commandos would need to take was a series of steep climbs and descents up and down Sark's cliffs and valleys. A two-dimensional photograph or map would not give an accurate impression of the lay of the land.

As the commandos made their preparations, studying the intelligence they had, there was at least one German who had a premonition that the peace on the little paradise island of Sark might soon be shattered. Just five days before the commandos landed on Sark, Hitler made a three-hour speech to a conference attended by very senior Nazi officials. He was concerned about possible breaches in the Channel Islands' defences:

> Above all, I am grateful to the English for proving me right by their various landing attempts. It shows up those who think I am always seeing phantoms, who say, 'Well, when are the English coming? There is absolutely nothing happening on the coast – we swim every day, and haven't seen a single Englishman!'[13]

Hitler demanded that all the Channel Islands be turned into fortresses, and that the Atlantic Wall defences be strengthened.

Some of the weapons deployed by the Germans to defend Sark were truly fearsome. For example, the Wehrmacht put in place remote-controlled flamethrowers that would burn alive any attacking troops. In addition, the island was defended by thousands of mines, including the terrifying 'bouncing Betties', kilometres of barbed wire, armed patrols throughout the night, spotlights, anti-tank weapons and hundreds of well-trained, heavily armed infantrymen.

The first attempt to carry out Operation Basalt took place on the night of 19–20 September 1942, just six days after the disastrous Aquatint raid in which Gus March-Phillips had been killed. The original plan had been to go a day earlier, but was postponed due to bad weather. Though the weather wasn't perfect, Appleyard didn't want to delay a second time, so on the 19th the men readied themselves to raid Sark.

The raiders set out as usual from Portland on MTB *344*, commanded once again by Lieutenant Freddie Bourne. The departure from Portland was quite late, at nearly 2200hrs, as the boat headed out passing Alderney and the Casquets, scene of the earlier, highly successful SSRF raid. By midnight, land was spotted and identified incorrectly as Sark. The boat was, in fact, far off course and had seen various rocks, the small island of Herm and the much larger island of Guernsey. As Sergeant Stokes later put it, 'These sort of f***-ups happened all of the time.'[14] After correcting course, they approached Sark at the 'semi-silent' speed of 10 knots and reached the place where they intended to anchor only at 0135hrs. At that point they cut off the main engines entirely, slowing down to just 5 knots on the auxiliary engine.

But now the sea turned against them. The swell began to rise, and what Appleyard later referred to as 'patches of con-fused sea' made the going very difficult. The boat was pulled away by a very fast-moving stream in the sea, and they esti-mated that they'd not be able to successfully anchor in the right place until 0300hrs. Five hours had passed since leaving Portland. As they needed to begin their return voyage no later than 0330hrs in order to reach the safety of Portland before daybreak, it was no longer possible to complete the mission. In addition to that, the strong winds and 'confused sea' meant that the tiny Goatley landing craft may not have successfully made the short trip back and forth from the MTB to the shore.

Stokes wrote:

Our life was operating out of small boats so we knew how to read the weather and the sea, and on this occasion we could sense a number of things that didn't feel right. There was a strong wind, very strong current and big swell. Simply to get into a position from which we could get ashore would have taken us until about 3am and we knew that we needed to have the operation completed and be heading home at 03.30hrs.[15]

Appleyard then took the painful decision to abort the mission, and the boat sailed back to England, arriving in Portland Harbour by 0530hrs. The men were debriefed and returned to their billets at Anderson Manor. Stokes probably spoke for all the men when he later wrote: 'This was how it was sometimes, in fact more often than not, and if you were going to risk the lives of men then it takes as much courage to abort an operation as it does to give the thumbs up and to proceed with it.'[16]

This first abortive raid on Sark was not without value. They'd circled the island, and learned more about the sea there, its currents and the dangers they would face navigating those waters. When they came back, they would be better prepared to make a perfect landing on Sark.

On that same morning, as the commandos returned to Portland, Obergefreiter Hermann Weinreich and four of his comrades from the Wehrmacht's Pioneers (combat engineers) were transferred from Guernsey to Sark. Their job there was to fix a boom defence across the entrance of Creux Harbour on the eastern coast of the island. This defence consisted of two buoys, 1.5m high, which sink about half-way down into the water, and connected at the top and bottom by a thick wire strand, running into rings. This project, like all the other aspects of the Atlantic Wall, seemed designed to deter a full-on, frontal assault by enemy troops, and would not in the least have affected a commando raid. As it turned out, Weinreich would only have two weeks in Sark, and would spend the rest of the war in British captivity. Two members of his team had only two weeks left to live.

A day after the raiders came back, on 21 September, Appleyard had a meeting in London with 'M'. At this point, the SSRF had two masters, both the SOE and Combined Operations, headed by Mountbatten. It was their first meeting after March-Phillips' death, and Appleyard was now running the SSRF on his own.

It is not known what Appleyard and 'M' discussed, but within a few days Appleyard sent a handwritten note marked 'MOST SECRET' to his commander (addressed to SOO, HMS *Southwick*), in which he wrote:

> I should like to have another shot at operation 'BASALT' on the night of 3rd/4th Oct., or failing that the first suitable subsequent night. M.T.B. 344 would be used, sailing from Portland. If you concur, would you please send the necessary signals … Apart from the date, I think these will be exactly as before.

Appleyard, though actually commanding the SSRF at this time, was still signing his reports as '2nd in Command' in honour of his close friend, the late March-Phillips.

A week after the first attempt on Sark, 'M' paid a visit to Anderson Manor, meeting all the men in the SSRF and presumably the new additions from No. 12 Commando as well. A few days later, Appleyard's commanding officer at HMS *Southwick* scrawled on the bottom of his message: '3rd Oct. is one day after last quarter of moon. Propose to lay on.' The raiders had needed to wait until the moon was in the right phase. This was confirmed on 1 October in a message from the base commander in Portsmouth on 1 October, just two days before the raid. The message was concise: 'Carry out OPERATION 'BASALT' night of 3rd/4th October or first suitable subsequent night.'

Operation Basalt was now set for a second attempt.

POINTE CHÂTEAU

The second try at Operation Basalt began on the evening of 3 October 1942. It had been a hot day in Sark and the night was typical for autumn in the Channel Islands – 'thick mist at sea level but a starry night above'.[1] Bright moonlight would shine from around 0300hrs, just around the time the commandos needed to make their escape. The weather, the moon and the tides all made it a good night for a commando raid on Sark.

That morning, the men were briefed on the raid planned for that night and given the afternoon off to rest or make any personal preparations. In the evening, they were taken from their base at Anderson Manor down to Portland. Among those joining them this time was a Captain Warre of the ME Raiding Group, though it appears that he stayed on board the boat the whole time.

At just after 1900hrs MTB 344 left Portland under the command once again of Lieutenant Freddie Bourne. They departed three hours earlier than the previous attempt, so one lesson had been learned. On the journey out to Sark, the men gathered around the Goatley in the back of the MTB. Because of the engine noise, they had to shout to one another to be heard. They wore lifejackets, but still felt the cold of the night. As Anders Lassen remembered, 'a cigarette would be wonderful, but they had to do without as the Germans might see a light. Apple went round the deck giving his instructions to the group. His foot was not alright yet, but thought he would be able to manage.'[2]

Though the officers had already been briefed and shown the aerial photos and model of Sark, it was only halfway through their nearly four-hour journey to the island that Appleyard told the men exactly where they were going. They would be landing on Sark, and specifically on its eastern side on the Hog's Back, which they would need to climb and then walk straight north on a path leading inland. Bourne had to pilot the boat through German mines, but was aided by the fact that it was high tide and the boat had a shallow draught.

Three hours into their journey when they were just 6km off the southern tip of Sark, they were spotted. They saw a signal from the German forces on the island asking who they were. Apple replied using a signal lamp (known as an Aldis) saying that they were a German vessel and intended to shelter in Dixcart Bay for the night. The ruse worked and no alarm was sounded.[3] The MTB came round to the eastern side of Sark and approached the Hog's Back.

Sark is surrounded on all sides by steep cliffs, making the choice of where to land a difficult one. The easiest place to land a small boat on Sark, then and now, is Creux Harbour. But intelligence reports suggested that it was guarded by armed customs officials and the tunnel connecting it to the road that leads up the hill was gated. A barracks for German soldiers was being built there as well. The commandos didn't have the easy option, then. They'd need another route up to the top of the cliff.

Appleyard's post-action report reviewed his reasoning behind the choice to make the landing not on a beach, with a relatively easy climb to the top, but at the foot of a very steep cliff leading up to the Hog's Back, a narrow headland jutting out to sea. He wrote:

Very recent air cover had reported a new possible defence position on the top of the cliff at the end of PTE. CHÂTEAU.

This position would undoubtedly have been able to cover both DIXCART BAY and DERRIBLE BAY, the two obvious landing points, and might have made re-embarkation from either of these two bays difficult after an alarm had been given.

This was unfortunate, as either bay offered relatively easy places to land and both had well-defined routes inland. As Appleyard wrote:

DIXCART BAY offered an easy landing on a steep shingle beach at all states of the tide and a subsequent easy and level route inland up the DIXCART valley, whilst a landing in DERRIBLE BAY could be on sand at anything except high water and would be followed by an ascent up a steep and difficult cliff path in the N.E. corner of the Bay to the high land beyond.

But because of that 'possible defence position' at the end of the Hog's Back, Dixcart Bay and Derrible Bay were ruled out. There seemed to be no good place to land the commandos, but as Appleyard noted – 'except for the fact that an old guide book had stated that it was possible to make a long and difficult climb down the cliff at the very tip of the HOGS BACK, i.e., PTE. CHÂTEAU, to examine some caves at sea level'. The 'old guide book' was certainly *La Trobe's Guide to Sark*.

Appleyard judged that a machine-gun position on top of the cliff would be unlikely to threaten commandos climbing straight up; the Germans would be focussing their attention on the two bays on either side of the Hog's Back. And a climb directly up the cliff would have the element of surprise, as this seemed the most difficult way to reach the top. The commandos had been training for precisely this sort of thing and if anyone could make the climb, they could. For a man who took pleasure in dangling from a cliff at the end of a rope hundreds of feet above the sea in order to gather some birds' eggs, the climb from Pointe Château was an obvious choice.

Nevertheless, Appleyard needed a Plan B. He wrote:

> If the cliff should then prove unscaleable, or if the landing should not appear wise owing to the exposed nature of the head to sea and swell, a second landing would be made at the foot of the cliff path in DERRIBLE BAY. It later transpired that DIXCART BAY has lately been mined and that DERRIBLE BAY is thought to have been mined.[4]

Appleyard's assumption that the two bays may have been mined may not have been correct. The German prisoner they would capture on Sark that night later insisted that the mining of the beaches just wasn't possible. He said he'd never heard of minefields on Sark's beaches, and insisted that salt water would render the mines useless.

The main concern, the one that actually determined where the commandos would land that night, was that German machine-gun emplacement. As it turned out, there were no Germans sitting on top of the Hog's Back headland. What the aerial reconnaissance had spotted was almost certainly a decommissioned eighteenth-century cannon, one of several placed on the island to defend it against Napoleon's armies. It can still be seen today at the end of the Hog's Back.

As the Little Pisser approached Sark, Appleyard ordered Bourne to wait about 300m offshore. He was told to wait for a couple of hours. If the commandos did not return on time, it would mean that they had been captured or killed, and Bourne was to return to England. At 2312hrs the twelve commandos boarded the Goatley and they paddled silently towards shore.

The landing did not go exactly as planned. Though Appleyard would later report that 'Lassen acted very ably as bowman and the party was disembarked dryshod', the truth was rather different, as he acknowledged in the same report. After landing their little canvas and wood Goatley:

It was then discovered that the landing had been made on a small rock island off the point and it was necessary for the party to re-embark and make a fresh landing on the mainland. Two members of the party, however, swam the small intervening gully and assisted from the shore in the second landing.[5]

Apparently the water temperature around Sark in early October is not particularly cold, and only a little below the August maximum.

Within a few minutes all the men were re-landed. With all the commandos now ashore, Second Lieutenant Graham Salter Young was given charge of the Goatley. He 'hauled her off the rock into deep water with the kedge line, whilst the bowline was firmly secured above H.W. mark by means of belying the rope and using a grapnel,' reported Appleyard.[6] The rest of the men were now ashore.

They knew that there was a German searchlight placed on top of an old mill near the centre of the island. But it had not been turned on them. They looked up the very steep cliffs and saw no lights at all, nor any signs of barbed wire.[7] 'All you could hear,' wrote Sergeant Stokes, 'was the wind and the noise of the sea.'[8]

THE HOG'S BACK

Appleyard checked that each man had the equipment he would need. Everyone synchronised their watches. The men had chosen their own weapons, carrying Sten guns, .45 Colt revolvers, and the famous Fairbairn–Sykes fighting knife.

Someone had to quickly scale the cliff to see if there really was a German machine-gun position there, and Anders Lassen volunteered for the job. While he raced up towards the top, the other ten commandos followed more slowly. Normally, it might have been Appleyard in the lead, but his foot was still suffering from the injury he'd sustained in the successful raid on the Casquets Lighthouse just a few weeks before. 'The ascent was very steep and difficult for the first 150ft, and made dangerous by shale and loose rock and the darkness,' reported Appleyard, 'but the gradient then eased and the route ended up steep gullies of seathrift and rock to the top of Hogs Back.'[1] Stokes said it 'was a very difficult climb that eased toward the top. What we thought might be a tough scramble was a full climb and really hard work.'[2]

It wasn't until midnight that all the commandos reached the top. They were pleased to notice that their MTB, which could be seen quite clearly from the foot of the cliff, was invisible from the top against the darker background of the sea. Gunner Redborn reported that upon reaching the clifftop the men found 'barbed wire entanglements. The stillness of the night was only broken by the cry of a seagull or when the wire was snapped with cutters. We fumbled around the whole time in the dark …'[3] According to one report, upon reaching the top the commandos covered the barbed wire they found there with luminous paint in order to facilitate their return by the same route.[4]

Several accounts of the raid emphasise the silence on Sark, with the only sounds normally heard being the crashing of waves and the cries of seagulls. Even the cutting of barbed wire could have alerted attentive German patrols, had there been any such patrols in the area. Though Sark can be quite silent, the sounds of waves crashing against the shore and of the strong winds that often batter the island can be quite noisy. The commandos thought that every sound they were making as they toppled loose rock from the cliffs to the sea, or cut barbed wire, could be heard kilometres away. In fact this was almost certainly not the case.

Later on that night, as they smashed glass and broke down doors, they still managed to avoid being heard by the Germans. Because of Sark's rich topography, with deep valleys in some parts, sound travels in strange ways. As one current local resident put it, in some parts of the island there are virtual 'sound tunnels' which allow voices to carry for enormous distances. The commandos benefitted from Sark's unusual acoustics during their entire time on the island.

As the commandos assembled on top of the cliff, Lassen returned and reported back that he had found no defence post along the whole of the Hog's Back. Lassen had gone about 100m inland after cutting through barbed wire. He'd found no signs of mines either. The commandos found the nineteenth-century cannon that aerial reconnaissance had reported as a possible German machine-gun nest. It was a relief to all that this was the case. 'This was good news,' wrote Stokes, 'as we would either have had to deal with it quietly' – no doubt using their special commando skills, especially with the knife – 'or go around it'.

As they assembled at the clifftop, relieved to find no German machine-gun nest there, the men were startled when a seagull suddenly flew up and away calling. To their relief, it was just the one. Had there been more, the Germans might have noticed. They cut through a second line of barbed wire, when Lassen was surprised to see Captain Pinckney digging at something in the ground. He assumed Pinckney had found a mine. But when he stopped digging, Lassen saw him put a plant in his pocket. 'Pinckney was crazy, everywhere he picked grass!!' Lassen later wrote about the amateur botanist:[5]

> Pinckney was a fanatical vegetarian. Pinckney cooked grass and plants together … it was important for soldiers he said, to like what nature gave you to eat. When he approached with a plant in his hand men ran away, afraid of being used as guinea pigs.[6]

Appleyard whispered that the commandos should move on. Lassen had the best night vision, so he was first in the column as they walked north along the path on the Hog's Back. Appleyard warned them to all be careful as they approached their primary target, Petit Dixcart, situated in a little valley less than half a kilometre from the clifftop overlooking Pointe Château.

According to Appleyard's father, 'As Geoff reached the top of the cliff after a stiff climb, and cautiously peered over the edge, he was horrified to see the vague silhouettes of a number of German soldiers about fifty yards away.' Appleyard:

> … waited for some minutes in the hope that they would move on and then decided that here was an ideal opportunity to eliminate a complete German patrol and probably get a few prisoners as well. He therefore crawled stealthily towards the enemy and when he had shortened the range so that it was impossible for the men to miss, he prepared to give the order to fire. Then a doubt crossed his mind. None of the figures ahead of him had moved since he first saw them, nor had they

made a sound. He decided to investigate and crawled nearer and nearer. Then to their amazement his men heard him chuckle, stand up and call them forward. They found him examining a row of perfectly dressed dummies used by the island garrison for target practice![7]

In some reports of the raid, Petit Dixcart is referred to as the commandos' 'primary target', though it's not entirely clear why this would be the case. There is no evidence that the British had any agents on Sark, nor did aerial reconnaissance give much information about where the Germans were based. Petit Dixcart is a large private home with landscaped gardens today and was much the same in 1942. It is some distance from the centre of the island where the Germans had put their headquarters and Appleyard would have realised this from his earlier visits to Sark with his family. So why make it the primary target for the raid?

The answer is obvious as you walk down the path on the Hog's Back leading from the seaside cliffs to the main part of the island. Petit Dixcart is quite simply the first sizeable building, or group of buildings, you will come across. It was not unreasonable to expect that the Germans would use a building of this size to house their troops, even if there was no prior intelligence of this. 'The route inland was pretty rough going through really thick prickly gorse and bracken,' wrote Stokes.

Although he made no mention of the dummies he mistook for a German patrol in his official report, Appleyard did admit that as the commandos moved along the ridge of the Hog's Back they came up to 'what was thought to be a Nissen hut and wireless mast', which:

> … were observed beside the ruins of an old mill. This was immediately attacked and it was discovered that the wireless mast was a flagpole and the supposed Nissen hut was the butts and targets of a range, the firing point of which was some 200 yds to the North.[8]

It is not entirely clear what Appleyard means by 'attacked' but presumably no one fired their weapons. The Germans were still completely unaware that any British soldiers had landed on Sark.

Appleyard led the way, with Pinckney bringing up the rear. Gunner Redborn was in the middle, walking with Anders Lassen, and he reported that they heard a German patrol coming. Lassen's biographer, Frithjof Saelen, told the story of what happened next:

> He at once lay down on the edge as did the others behind him. They could hear steps on the path. Suddenly six men came walking along. The Germans walked with their heads bent and heavy steps, four seemed as if they were sleepy. Must be a gang coming off duty he thought.
>
> One of the soldiers swore terribly as he passed Anders, the others laughed. The leader stopped the group for a moment and said something in German. Anders caught the words 'the Channel' and 'the British'. They were nearly caught but they now knew that the Germans were on watch. They had been very lucky, next time it might not be so good. They were more careful now. They slowed down their pace after this meeting.
>
> After a while they lay down again, they had revolvers and Sten guns ready. One of the soldiers had heard something, they waited for a while, but nobody appeared. And so it went on slowly, every now and then they heard branches snap and stones kicked, and they were very tense, things grew in their imagination, and it was very difficult to see in the darkness. The one good thing was that it was equally hard for the Germans to spot them.
>
> Apple did not trust the gang that had passed, they might go out to the line where the barbed wire was cut, he could only hope they might not see it in the dark. It was now time that they got into a house somewhere, they could see a few houses about 100 metres away. Apple sent two men along to

reconnoitre, at last they signalled all clear and hidden by hedges and bushes they crept along. The houses were empty, it seemed as if they had been robbed, Anders went through all of them – you could never trust to chance with the Germans, but he found nobody. 'There must be some reason,' he thought, and picked up a few papers. 'This house must belong to people who evacuated to England.'

Apple considered that explanation was reasonable, but there was no object in delaying there, they must get on. Without a sound they went across the small valley towards a house which stood all by itself in the middle of a lawn.[9]

An hour and fifteen minutes had already passed since they'd reached the top of the cliffs. Every minute now counted, as they needed to be off the island within a couple of hours in order to make a safe getaway under cover of darkness to England. And of course every minute they traipsed around in the gorse and bracken, the chances of being discovered by a German patrol rose.

II

MRS PITTARD

The commandos now began to move towards their secondary target, a large, isolated private home called La Jaspellerie. Though later reports claimed the British had intelligence that the house 'contained a number of Germans', it seems more likely that it followed the primary target at Petit Dixcart because it was the next closest building in proximity to the Hog's Back.[1] Look at a normal map of Sark and the two buildings, Petit Dixcart and La Jaspellerie, seem practically next door to each other. They appear to be only 200m apart, but when you're actually there, on the ground, you realise that they are separated by a deep and thickly wooded valley, with a stream running down it.

It was now 0135hrs. Moving about in pitch darkness and silence was taking a very long time. The commandos had now been on Sark for more than two hours. Time was running short; soon Freddie Bourne would have to take the Little Pisser back to England, with or without the commandos on board. When they reached La Jaspellerie, on top of the cliff overlooking the sea, Appleyard ordered most of the men to remain behind under cover, while three of the party toured the house and the outbuildings, one of which contained a horse. They tried all the doors and windows on the ground floor, but these were all locked. Some French windows on the south-east side of the house appeared to be easy to force open, so they broke in at 0150hrs. Appleyard and Corporal Flint moved into the building.[2]

Mrs Frances Noel Pittard, then 40 years old, was the widow of the island's doctor. Frances was born in England, where her father was a Royal Navy commander, but she had lived in Sark most of her life. Her family, the Mardons, owned a business in Bristol and property on Sark. To get a sense of how prominent the Mardons were on Sark, one need only visit St Peter's Church on Sark today. There's a large and beautiful stained glass window commemorating Frances' mother. Her older sister Sibyl also lived on Sark. Unlike Frances, she billeted German troops in her home.

Frances had been married for more than a decade to Dr Marmaduke Pittard, who was very well liked by the islanders. According to Richard Le Tissier, 'while treating the less well-off, he would usually forgo his consultation fee and settle for a fresh lobster or a few pounds of new potatoes.' But Dr Pittard retired in 1939. A replacement was found for him and he and Frances moved from the traditional doctor's residence at Le Vieux Clos to La Jaspellerie.

When the islanders were given a chance to evacuate before the Germans arrived, Dr Pittard's replacement fled in a private boat. Pittard himself, old and nearly blind, agreed to return to his duties as the island's doctor. After a short while, he was replaced by a doctor from Jersey, who proved unpopular and resigned. Guernsey doctors would then come over for weekly visits, but this was unsatisfactory. Eventually the Dame persuaded the Germans to provide medical care for the islanders.

Dr Pittard died on 15 July 1942, leaving Frances living alone in a large and isolated home overlooking the cliffs.

They found no Germans in the house. The intelligence about this, like the machine-gun emplacement at the top of Hog's Back, proved to be inaccurate. Lassen remembered that:

> The house was big, so they lay down and looked it over carefully; they saw nothing to indicate that there may be Germans living in the house or outbuildings, but it would be strange if no Germans were there so they had better count on that possibility. One of the soldiers broke a window standing on the back of another man, the hooks were unfastened and Anders was the next to go in, but it seemed quite empty. They pushed the doors open ready to fire, but the ground floor was quite empty, not a person and not a sound to be heard. They went on upstairs into a corridor. Apple lighted around with his torch, there were doors on each side, a soldier was at each door, ready on a sign from Apple to rush the rooms. Suddenly one of the doors opened, they saw an elderly woman in a nightgown, sleepy eyed and looking at them with astonishment.
>
> 'Is the house on fire?' she asked.

As Appleyard wrote in his report, 'A quick search of the house revealed the presence of only one woman (whose name can be had from M.I.19).' Her name was Mrs Pittard.

Appleyard ordered all his men outside of the house except for one, and over the course of about an hour, he interrogated Mrs Pittard. What followed was extraordinary; Mrs Pittard proved to be an extremely valuable source of information.

It is important to emphasise that this is not what always happened. There were occasions when commandos landed on other Channel Islands and were met with hostility or indifference by the locals. In Jersey in December 1943, Captain P.A. Ayton landed with a force of ten commandos and, like his predecessors on Sark, initially found no Germans. As John Nettles tells the story:

They knocked on the door of a farmhouse to see if they could get some information as to where enemy troops might be found. The Jersey lady who answered their midnight summons was anything but pleased to see these heavily armed men with blackened faces.

No Mrs Pittard [was] she. She was not particularly frightened, just quite annoyed. No she would not tell them where German troops were. The people on the farm down the road might be able to help so why didn't they just clear off and ask them.[3]

In her own defence the lady later claimed, rather implausibly, that she believed that the commandos were Germans who spoke very good English.

On Sark, a year earlier, Mrs Pittard put loyalty to Britain ahead of her personal safety in a genuine act of heroism. Here is Lassen's account of what happened:

Are there any Germans here, asked Apple. The woman looked at the soldiers' black faces and at their guns. 'No, I live here all alone, my husband died last June, so …'[4]

'All of a sudden she realised that she had only her nightgown on …

'Wait a moment,' she said, and went back to her room, put on some more clothes and came back.

'They went downstairs again, the lady took everything very easily and smiled when Apple apologised for having alarmed her, he asked if she would like to go back to England?

'No thank you,' she said, she had to take care of her animals and could not leave them. Apple agreed to that, so they all gathered in her drawing room and Mrs Pittard, as her name was, drew the curtains and lit a light.

'Had she got a map of Sark?' Yes, she would fetch it. While they were waiting, Anders looked around. In the corner, the breakfast table was laid for Sunday breakfast. There was English marmalade, some apples in a dish, but what was most interesting was a loaf of bread of a strange colour.[5]

Lassen continued:

> One of the men who had been posted outside to look out, now came in and said he had seen a light flutter on the second floor. Everyone turned to the staircase as the lady came back, she had only lit a match to find the map and had not thought it would show from the window. Anders went across to her with the loaf of bread and said he would take it away with him to have it analysed, but she begged him not to take all as it was all her ration for the week, so he took a small piece and put the rest back.

It was important to the British to learn as much as possible about life under German occupation. As the intelligence report submitted after the raid noted: 'Bread can now only be bought twice a week, and the ration is two loaves of about 2-lbs each, each week. The bread is very dark and coarse in quality. Sample has been submitted to M.I.10 for analysis.'[6] (MI10 was the branch of Military Intelligence responsible for weapons and technical analysis. And, apparently, bread.)

Lassen continued:

> Apple studied the map, asked for information as to belts of mines etc. They had not much time so would she point out as much as she knew. Apple marked everything she pointed out, but she said she knew very little about the German defences. She only knew that they had some kinds of guns in different places but had not the faintest idea of what types they were. She described everything as well as she could and Apple understood what she meant. She looked at the soldiers with curiosity. Where had they landed? Apple thought it would not matter if she knew. 'Hogs Back.'
>
> By the way did they know anything about the Germans sending British born men and their families to Germany? The soldiers did not know this, it had been done recently, so

she gave Apple the approximate numbers. Mrs Pittard also found the newspaper with the order signed by the German Commandant in Jersey.

'Is there anywhere in this neighbourhood where we can get prisoners?'

'Yes,' she replied, 'very close to this house, at Dixcart Hotel a bit further down in the valley,' there she said were about a dozen men from the 'Organisation Todt'. Apple nodded, he said he knew the place. Anders and Pinckney had been all over the house, they now came back with some odd things and said they would like to take away a little of everything, especially samples of food and medicines. Some of it was German made and the authorities in England would probably like to have a look at the things.

Now Apple looked at this watch, they shook hands with Mrs Pittard and wished her all the best when she suddenly remembered something. Could they let her family in England know that she was alright. Apple thought they could do so and asked her to write a few words. She wrote two letters and Apple took them and promised to post them in London. Now they all went. Anders was the last to leave. 'I am afraid we have broken one of your windows.' She thought that would not matter very much, but what if the Germans came and noticed it? She must say that the wind had broken it after he suggested, as they had recently had a gale, then he said goodbye and went after the others. It was getting late and Apple wondered if they could manage an attack on Dixcart Hotel and be back at the boat in time, all the same it would be a pity if they did not get at least one prisoner.[7]

Appleyard later wrote in his report:

This woman proved to be well educated and intelligent and to have lived in the Channel Islands all her life. Her father is an R.N.V.R. Captain at present resident in England, as is her daughter.

> Four of the most recent editions of the local Guernsey newspaper were obtained, also other pamphlets and documents of interest.[8]

Mrs Pittard struck Major Appleyard as being 'well educated and intelligent'. But later German reports described her as being 'a helpless and somewhat simple-minded woman', leading one to think that she may well have played a role when the Germans interrogated her. In any event, the commandos now had a target: the Annexe at the Dixcart Hotel. This was even closer to La Jaspellerie than Petit Dixcart was, just a couple of hundred metres away.

In the more than seven decades that have passed since Operation Basalt, many of the details of the raid remain obscure. Here is one example. As Appleyard put it in his official account of the raid:

> In view of the fact that the landing party had already been ashore more than an hour longer than the anticipated time, *one of the party* was sent off across country back to the landing craft to flash a signal to the M.G.B. [Motor Gun Boat] that everything was in order. As it happened, this man did not reach the landing craft until the rest of the party finally re-embarked, as he got badly held up in dense undergrowth.[9]

It was necessary to send a runner back on foot as the commandos apparently were not carrying any radio equipment. It is not clear how the commandos would signal to the MTB offshore.

Horace Stokes, in his memoir of the raid, confirmed Appleyard's account, writing that 'one of the party was going to leave us and make their way back to the coast in order to signal to the boat and let them know we were ok as we didn't want them buggering off without us'.[10] Both accounts agree that this is what happened – but who was this 'one of the party' sent away?

In an interview with historian Tom Keene many decades after the event, Corporal Edgar said it was him:

> I was ordered by Appleyard to hurry back to the cliff-top and to flash 'wait' as we had over-run our specified time and the boat might depart without us. In the moonlight I got lost in the whins [*sic*] and had to force my way, losing my belt with .45 colt in the process.[11]

Richard Le Tissier named Corporal Flint as the man sent to get word to Freddie Bourne to keep the Little Pisser waiting around a while longer. He wrote that Flint 'was sent back to the boat to tell the crew to wait another hour'.[12] Corporal Edgar disagrees, insisting that he 'was the Commando ordered by Major Appleyard to return to the clifftop and signal to the MTB "to wait"'.[13]

But according to Anders Lassen, it wouldn't have been either corporal. An officer, he remembered, 'offered to go back to the boat and tell them to wait another half hour. Apple told him to stay down there as there was no need for him to come back. He went round the hedge and in a moment he disappeared in the darkness.'[14]

That is one mystery about the raid, but there are more. Did Mrs Pittard tell the commandos where to go, or did she lead them to the Germans herself? And if she told them, did she name the Dixcart Hotel, or was she more specific, naming the Annexe? These two questions remain unanswered after seventy years – and they raise tantalising questions about what happened in the next few minutes. If Mrs Pittard walked them over to the hotel, she would have left a set of footprints that would later be found by the Germans, as some have argued. There are several different accounts of how the Germans discovered the role she played that night.

It seems unlikely that she would have joined the commandos at this point as the hotel was only a couple of minutes walk from her home and they knew their way around this part of the island. And for operational reasons, the last thing they needed at this point was a civilian in their team as they tried to move silently and quickly towards the Germans.

The other issue concerns the precision of the directions Mrs Pittard gave. If she told them that Germans were staying at the hotel but did not specify precisely where, the commandos would have needed that additional piece of information. Upon their return to England, Appleyard delivered his first report on the raid in which he said that 'on asking at the hotel, they were told that the Germans were living in the annexe'. Who could they have asked? The only people staying in the hotel at the time were two English ladies, Miss Duckett and Miss Page, who were the hotel's joint managers. When interrogated by the Germans after the raid, they insisted they had slept through everything – but that's exactly what they would have said.

The commandos did everything they could to stay silent and were largely successful, but their first encounter with a German soldier did end in a muffled cry. If Duckett and Page were light sleepers, and assuming that the German sentry was killed near their living quarters, they may well have been awakened. Before that the commandos had shattered glass at Mrs Pittard's house, but if that didn't alert the German sentry, it was unlikely to have been loud enough to awaken the sleeping ladies at the hotel. It turned out that the Germans, who were asleep in the Annexe, heard neither the broken glass nor the sound of their comrade being killed.

No evidence emerged after the war to indicate that Duckett and Page had actually been awake and given directions to Appleyard and his men, but it remains an intriguing possibility. After their deportation to Germany, they played leading roles in the community of deportees and were quite close to Mrs Pittard. Maybe this was a secret shared.

Appleyard's own later account revised his story, and he reported that, 'Acting on information given by this woman' – meaning Mrs Pittard – they learned 'there were a number of Germans billeted in the annexe of the DIXCART Hotel, but that there were no Germans in the DIXCART Hotel itself.' The short walk from La Jaspellerie to the Dixcart Hotel took the commandos through the hotel grounds, a point noted by Appleyard in a letter he later wrote to his younger brother. As the commandos approached the hotel, they were acutely aware of how much noise they had been making despite their thick, rubber-soled shoes, including breaking the glass at Mrs Pittard's house. They knew they had been spotted when their boat first approached Little Sark. They needed to move quickly now, and silently, as they crept up on their German prey.

ALL HELL BREAKS LOOSE

As the raiders approached the hotel, Appleyard sent Lassen and Redborn in first to reconnoitre the complex. Lassen was often the point man on this raid, as on others, having been the first to climb the cliff.

Obergefreiter Peter Oswald was on sentry duty, almost certainly positioned on top of the slope overlooking both the Dixcart Hotel and the attached Annexe. He was pacing back and forth, yawning and showing every sign of being tired and bored. The first signs of his presence were either steps the commandos heard on the path, or the shadow of his distinctive Wehrmacht helmet. In any event, they spotted him before he spotted them. The whole team hid behind bushes only a few metres away from the hotel. Lassen was sure it was a sentry they had seen; he would pace a bit, then stop and retrace his steps.

Lassen and Redborn returned to Appleyard to report. Appleyard ordered them to deal with the sentry. Lassen then told Redborn, 'You stay here', and went up ahead. Lassen pulled out his Fairbairn–Sykes fighting knife, also known as a commando knife. (Fairbairn and Sykes, both British captains, designed the knife based on their experience of close-quarter combat while they served in Shanghai as colonial police.) The knife was a deadly weapon, twin-edged and useful both for thrusting and throwing. Lassen was an expert at both.

Meanwhile, the other commandos crept ever closer and by now they could see the German sentry. Lassen listened carefully to the sentry's paces, calculating how long it would take him to do a complete round and turn. He could tell when the German was turning on his heel. As he waited, the moon came out and illuminated Lassen's face, causing him to take a few quick steps back into the bushes. The sentry paused for a moment, stopping his pacing. He had heard nothing, but he yawned. This was the moment Lassen chose to strike.

Coming up from behind the unsuspecting man, Lassen stabbed him between the shoulder blades using his knife. The other commandos heard a muffled sound, described variously as a cry, sigh, scream or groan. Whatever sound the dying Oswald made, Appleyard heard it and nodded; he knew that Lassen had taken care of the sentry.[1] Lassen dragged the dead *obergefreiter* behind a bush, leaving him there. Because of this, his body remained hidden for several hours and it was not until morning that the Germans found him.

Lassen returned to announce that he'd taken care of the sentry and the team could proceed. It was the first time he'd used his knife in combat and he was visibly shaken by it. It confirmed his preference for using a bow and arrow, and he regretted not having the other weapon with him.

Appleyard expected to find another sentry closer to the Annexe, but there was none. The path was now clear to do what the commandos had come to Sark for: to capture a German soldier and bring him back to England.[2] As the commandos approached the Dixcart Hotel's Annexe silently, five German soldiers slept inside. They were engineers ('pioneers' as the Wehrmacht called them), deployed only days earlier to Sark to prepare defences in the island's tiny harbour against any possible Allied landings. Previously they had been based on Guernsey, and before that, France. Their commander was Obergefreiter Hermann Weinreich, a married carpenter from Hemleben, a town in Prussia. The other four sleeping engineers were Unteroffizier August Bleyer, Gefreiter Heinrich Esslinger, Gefreiter Just and Gefreiter Klotz. They lived in conditions of relative luxury, each one sleeping in his own room.

Appleyard was concerned that there had been only one sentry and he was sure there would be others nearby. He ordered his men to enter the Annexe immediately as the building seemed unguarded. The hotel 'seemed absolutely dead,' recalled Lassen. 'The windows were all black and shut up.'[3] The Annexe was an extension to the old hotel, built of corrugated iron and consisting of a long, low corridor with cell-like rooms on each side. It remained standing for many years after the war, but has since been torn down.

According to the account published after the war by Lassen's mother, the commandos then rushed in:

> The door of the smaller house had gone crooked and they made an awful noise opening it. They rushed into the house and found that all the lights in the first room were on, which dazzled them so that they could hardly see a thing. Fortunately there was nobody there. They were rather surprised. At one end of the room there was a door which they watched carefully – it probably led to the rest of the house, they stood uncertainly waiting for a moment. The walls were covered with German notices, in a corner there were five rifles which meant that there must be six men counting the one that had been killed. Anders quietly crossed the floor and pushed open the opposite door, behind it was a passage with six doors.

Few things give a clearer indication of how secure and confident the German occupiers felt on Sark than this description. Not only were these soldiers far from the centre of the island and relatively close to the cliffs (in breach of orders), guarded by just one sentry, but they had left their rifles unguarded in a corner of a room while they went off to sleep in other rooms.

In many armies, soldiers are trained to sleep with their weapons, particularly if they are based in occupied and potentially hostile territory. What came next confirms the impression that a visit from the commandos was the very last thing any German soldier on Sark expected that night.

Appleyard gave the order for six of his men to position themselves in front of each of the six doors to the rooms. When he gave the signal, each man was to run into his assigned room. According to an account based on Lassen's diary:

Anders came into a room which was quite dark, found the window and then put on the light. A bed of iron stood out from the wall and a man lay in it. Anders pulled away the blanket and shook the German who smelt of perspiration, tobacco and perfume, and who was sound asleep. A little tickling with the knife helped to wake him, he opened his eyes and looked straight into Anders' black face. The man opened his mouth to shout but Anders hit him, he could not allow any noise. In haste he cut the sheet into strips and tied the man's hands, then he took a jug of water that was there and poured it on his face to revive him and examined the room, took some papers from the table and found a diary in the pocket of his uniform, from a hook he took a camera and threw it over his shoulder.

The German started to murmur, Anders was at once at his side and pushed him into the passage where he found Pinckney was having trouble with a prisoner. The Germans shouted and complained, they wanted to be dressed they said. Pinckney's prisoner looked evil, but he was obviously frightened. 'Shut up!' Pinckney shook him. It was no good. Apple and the others had prisoners, five in all, they all shouted and complained. It did not last long, the British used their fists, there was nothing else to be done, no time to get them to be quiet, in the end the Germans glared at them but did shut up. Redborn took care of the prisoners while the others went around and searched for papers and information to take away.[4]

Redborn's account of what happened is similar to Lassen's:

> I dashed into the room assigned to me and, while I was fumbling around in the dark, I heard loud snoring. I managed to turn the light on and saw a bed with a German sleeping on it. The first thing I did was to draw the curtains and pull the bedclothes off him. Half-asleep, he pulled them back over him. I took the blankets off him again and sleepily he opened his eyes. When he saw my black face he was terrified.
>
> I didn't break the silence. I knew that as long as he was terrified, he could neither talk nor act. Then I hit him under the chin with a knuckleduster and tied him up. Next I combed the room for papers, cameras and such like. After having got him on his feet I pushed him, still quite dazed, out into the corridor. There already stood Captain Pinckney, Andy and the others, with six prisoners altogether.[5] We had some difficulty with the prisoners. They kept shouting and complaining that they weren't allowed to put any decent clothes on; they were attired in the most varied assortment of togs. Helped by some blows, they became quieter – at least we thought so – and I was ordered to keep an eye on them while the others searched the rooms once more.

Both accounts mention the tying of the prisoners' hands. In Lassen's account, the tying seems improvised, done quickly, with the materials at hand – namely the German's bedsheets. Redborn's account is less clear about all of this, though it sounds more premeditated. Appleyard's post-action report made no mention of the binding of hands. The issue of the tying of the prisoners' hands will become a central part of the story of Operation Basalt, and these are the first references to this having happened.

The five prisoners were now together, some or all of them with their hands tied, in a wide range of clothing, including nightshirts, but none in proper army uniform. While they were guarded, some of the commandos went through their rooms collecting everything they could find that might be of interest to British Military Intelligence. These included weapons, pay books and other papers.

It was now time to take the prisoners outside and assemble them under cover of nearby trees. They would then begin the walk back down to the waiting Goatley and the trip back to England. As Redborn told the story, 'That done, we took the prisoners outside. The moment the last German stepped out of the house it started.'[6] Until this point, the mission seemed to have been a virtual repeat of Operation Dryad, the Casquets Lighthouse raid. The German soldiers who had been captured were hardly elite troops, as shown by the ease with which they were captured. Their state of complete unpreparedness included leaving their rifles stacked in another room while they slept. But what happened next took the commandos by surprise. The German soldiers apparently assumed that they were under attack from a much larger force. Perhaps the English were trying to retake Sark, or maybe this was just another very large commando raid, such as the one on Dieppe. But as the prisoners were gathered together outside, they realised in the moonlight that there were just ten commandos – and according to some accounts, only seven – surrounding them.

If there were only seven commandos at the Annexe with the German prisoners, it raises the question of what happened to all the others. One was guarding the Goatley down by the water and another was on his way to signal to Freddie Bourne on the Little Pisser that the men were on their way back. That should have left ten men to guard the five German prisoners. Some authors have speculated that Appleyard may have sent three men along to guard the route back to Pointe Château, but this seems unlikely. The discredited report by Leslie W. 'Red' Wright claimed that he was one of the men and that he had gone off to bring back a Polish SOE operative who'd been hiding on Sark.

Looking back at what happened that night, it's hard to know for sure. But it is possible that the commandos later claimed that there were just seven of them guarding five prisoners in order to emphasise why the Germans thought they had a chance, and to make what happened next seem like more of a fair fight. In all likelihood, it was now ten commandos with their five prisoners at this point. The Wehrmacht men were still outnumbered, but they had the advantage of the fact that there were another 300 or so heavily armed German infantrymen only a shout away.

According to the German report after the raid, it was Gefreiter Klotz who first realised that it might be possible to escape and sound the alarm. He 'was able to shed his handcuffs; he knocked down the British soldier guarding him and escaped into the darkness', they noted.[7] He not only ran away, but began shouting for help. For some reason, though the commandos had managed to tie their prisoners' hands, no one thought to gag them. This would not have been an issue on the previous raid on the Casquets Lighthouse; the only German soldiers there were the ones who were captured and their cries for help would have been heard by no one. But on tiny Sark, a German soldier shouting for help would be heard by his comrades.

Thanks to Klotz, it was now only a matter of time until the German garrison would be awakened. The mission, and the commandos' very lives, were now in danger. Gefreiter Klotz, it turned out, was the only German soldier to escape that evening unscathed. According to some reports, he was also the only one of the prisoners who was completely naked at the time. Following his example, the other German soldiers began shouting as well and Appleyard gave an order to silence them. But according to Lassen, things just got worse: 'The Germans went completely wild, they kicked the British and all the time shouted and swore as loudly as they could.'

Lassen, Redborn and Pinckney were in the thick of it:

Redborn's prisoner got his hands free and nearly managed to escape but Redborn tripped him up, knocked him down and sat on him. Anders had two prisoners, they tried to kick him on his shins and all were now struggling. Pinckney's German had also got his hands free, he stood next to Anders and kicked him at the back of his knees so that he fell, Pinckney was over him but he rolled away.[8]

Another of the Germans, Gefreiter Just, who was slightly wounded, also managed to escape. This left just three prisoners still in the hands of the British soldiers. According to Lassen's account, Appleyard gave the command: 'If they escape – shoot!' He added that:

Pinckney tried to catch his prisoner again but he got away and ran screaming towards the hotel. Anders saw Pinckney following him and then a shot was heard. Now it could be seen that Redborn was having a lot of trouble with his German. The man was bigger and stronger than he was and they were fighting in a flower bed, and Redborn felt he could not hold him, the man got away from him but Redborn caught him by the leg, but he fell on top of Redborn and started strangling him. Something had to be done so Redborn took his revolver and shot him.

Anders was still holding his two prisoners, they kicked him and shouted. His hands could no longer hold them. He too had to use a revolver. When one of them fell the other became quiet, so Anders shook him and told him he would also be shot unless he remained quiet, the man was scared and said he would do anything he was told.[9]

Redborn, who had command of one of the prisoners, later said:

I didn't quite realise what was happening, I was having so much trouble with my prisoner. He had freed his hands – we were struggling – and he was getting away from me. Then I bowled him over with a rugby tackle. We rolled over and he got free again. He was a much bigger fellow than I was, but I managed to knock him over again, and we lay struggling among some cabbage plants.

Confirming Lassen's account of Appleyard's order, he recalled:

One of the officers shouted loud enough for his voice to be heard above the din, 'If they try to get away – then shoot them!'

Captain Pinckney's prisoner broke free and set off towards the hotel, shouting at the top of his voice. Captain Pinckney chased him and a shot rang out.

I had had more than enough with my prisoner. I couldn't manage him and so I had to shoot him – and I found that the others were doing the same with their prisoners, except Andy who was still holding on to two prisoners. More shots sounded – and shouting and screaming, a terrible row, and lights began to come on in various parts of the hotel.

One wonders which hotel Redborn is referring to. The adjacent Dixcart Hotel was unoccupied by German troops at this time; the only residents were its managers, Misses Duckett and Page. They would later claim to have slept through it all, although if they were busy turning on lights in the hotel this was clearly not the case. The nearby Stocks Hotel is less than 100m away and German soldiers were almost certainly billeted there.

Redborn continued:

Andy, who had now got rid of his prisoners, wanted to go and throw grenades in through the windows, but Major Appleyard said, 'No, keep them! We might need them later on.' But now the Germans started to tear out of the hotel, and as soon as we knew there were a lot of them, we preferred to run for it. We had still got one prisoner who had seen what had happened to the others, and he was petrified and did everything he was told.[10]

It seems as though Pinckney's prisoner was actually shot by accident. Appleyard said as much in his report after the raid, noting that one of the prisoners 'was accidentally shot in an attempt to silence him by striking him with the butt of a revolver'.[11] According to one report, 'He hit his prisoner with the barrel of his pistol, not the butt – and forgetting his finger was on the trigger, blew the top of the German's head off'.[12]

The prisoners' shouts and the gunfire had awakened the German soldiers at the Stocks Hotel nearby. As Appleyard reported, 'There were answering shouts from the direction in which the prisoners had attempted to escape and sounds of a verbal alarm being given.'[13]

In the decades that have passed, it has become harder to sort out precisely what happened in those few minutes outside the Dixcart Hotel Annexe. Redborn claimed to have shot his prisoner, and it's generally conceded that Pinckney accidentally killed his, though some accounts claim it was Dudgeon who killed his prisoner. Sergeant 'Tim' Robinson told his family that *he* shot one of the Germans.

All that is known for certain is that two of the German engineers, Unteroffizier August Bleyer and Gefreiter Heinrich Esslinger, were shot, and the sentry, Obergefreiter Peter Oswald, was knifed by Lassen. One of the German soldiers stationed in Guernsey, Hauptmann Albert Engel, recounted the story to his grandson, saying:

> That he met the man who was stabbed. Actually, he was only hit with the tip of the knife in the back of his head, but enough to be unconscious and left for dead. Because of the shots fired at the other German prisoners, the men of the commando only wanted to leave the island as fast as possible. The men who tried to escape actually ran into barbed wire and that's when they got shot.[14]

The number of men who were shot by the commandos remains something of a mystery. Based on the evidence available today, it seems it was just the two, Bleyer and Esslinger, who are now buried in Guernsey. But Appleyard's report after the battle talked of four German casualties (not counting the sentry). He wrote about one German who:

> … was caught almost immediately by his guard, but after a scuffle again escaped, still shouting, and was shot. Meanwhile, three of the other prisoners seizing the opportunity of the noise and confusion also started shouting and attacking their guards. Two broke away and both were shot immediately. The third, although still held, was accidentally shot in an attempt to silence him by striking him with the butt of a revolver.[15]

It's not only the number of Germans shot that remains a matter of controversy, but also the number taken prisoner. Today it is known that it was just the one, Obergefreiter Hermann Weinreich, who surrendered. But some reports speak of two German prisoners being taken down to the boat, though by all accounts only one reached England.

It seems clear now that the only Germans left alive were the two who had succeeded in running away, one of them injured and the other naked, and Obergefreiter Hermann Weinreich who had the good sense to refuse to resist when confronted with the commandos' determination and ruthlessness.

Curiously, Weinreich's decision to surrender to the commandos and not put up a fight was glossed over in the official German report. General Müller, commander of the 319 Infantry Division, included Weinreich in his list of engineers who 'attempted to escape despite the fact they were handcuffed. Their behaviour meets the standard expected of a German soldier.'

Meanwhile, Corporal Edgar had got lost on his way to signal the boat, but heard the shots. As he told Tom Keene many years later: 'I discovered there was very, very, thick gorse in front of me – shocking sharp gorse and so I just dived into it and forced myself through it I hear: bang-bang, bang-bang, bang-bang, bang-bang and I said to myself: Oh, the boys have met up with them.'[16]

And an introspective Horace Stokes would write in his memoir about what had happened in those few minutes in the moonlight on Sark:

Years after the war I have had time to reflect on these moments and situations like this are rarely understood by anyone who has never been in such a position. We were by now a small team of ten men, a long way from home on an enemy held Island miles away from our only transport facing a far superior force.

Anyone who has handled prisoners under combat condi- tions a long way from home on the enemy's doorstep will know how hard this is. Especially when your prisoners know that you are outnumbered and outgunned, and that their lives are about to change forever one way or another. People can react to this in many different ways, some are subdued, which is what you hope for, others you know will fight. Once all hell breaks loose there is only one way to deal with this it's to be aggressive and controlling right from the start. It's known as the shock of capture. You can't f*** about.

Our job wasn't to fight the whole Island, our mission was to get prisoners home alive. By now everyone was being alerted to our position and we had only seconds in which to decide what to do. In the chaos two more German soldiers were killed leaving two who we were going to take back to England. Both of these men had been properly restrained with their hands tied. One of them was completely subdued, the other struggled wildly in response to the loud and approaching sounds of his fellow comrades who were now heading in our direction.

> We were told to bugger off and make haste back to the boat. I moved toward the front of the party with two [of] us forcibly taking control of the first POW [prisoner of war]. What seemed like a few seconds later we heard an almighty ruckus behind us and another shot was fired. We managed to recover one of the prisoners [Obergefreiter Weinreich] safely back to England where he provided a great deal of information.[17]

Weinreich was described in one account as being 'an unsoldierly specimen with thick glasses' who was so frightened that he collapsed and Lassen needed to carry him part of the way.[18]

Incredibly, amidst the chaos and violence in the hotel, Bruce Ogden-Smith grabbed a souvenir – a glass ashtray produced by the Guernsey Brewery Company, which he stuffed down his jacket and took back home.[19]

The commandos had now been on Sark for more than three hours. The man they'd sent to alert Freddie Bourne not to leave without them had got lost. Although he was unaware of this, Appleyard certainly realised that time was of the essence. Furthermore, the Germans now knew the commandos were on the island and were almost certainly in hot pursuit.

According to several accounts, at this stage the commandos had two prisoners with them, though only one finally made it to the boat. They heard the Germans shouting and, according to Lassen, bullets whizzed past them in the night. While the Germans may have been awakened, they hadn't a clue where the commandos were or where they were going.

Lassen's biographer described their escape, retracing their steps back down the valley and up again towards Petit Dixcart, then up on to the path on the Hog's Back, racing south to the clifftop overlooking the sea:

> They made their way towards Petit Dixcart, the paths were uneven and in many places obstructed by bushes and shrubs. They could hear Germans shouting and coming behind them,

the British rushed on down the slope and forced their way through the bushes in the dark. The branches tore at their faces and the thorns made them bleed, but they escaped as fast as they could. Pinckney had his hands on Anders' prisoner while Anders himself was the last man of the group. He helped another of the soldiers who was having great trouble with his prisoner, the man's face was completely white and his eyes stood out of his head he could hardly breathe, and suddenly he collapsed, so Anders had now to carry the German.[20]

Redborn's version is similar:

Didn't we run! We ran till every step hurt, not in an orderly fashion but in a kind of open patrol formation – and as fast as we possibly could. It was difficult to run along the uneven path which was in many places covered by brambles and thorns. We were pursued all the way. Andy came last because he was covering our retreat, and because he was helping a chap named Smith who had a job to get his breath. Andy was holding him round his arms.[21]

At last we got up to the Hog's Back – a hard climb. From here we could look down across the steep slope to the sea. Then we slithered down to the boat as fast as we could. We could hear the Germans coming after us down the slope. Hurriedly we got into the boat and reached the motor torpedo boat. They had been on the point of giving us up and sailing away.[22]

It took the commandos about twenty-five minutes to reach the clifftop with their prisoner in tow. By this time the moon had risen and there was a clear sky. Anyone looking for the British boat would see it, though fortunately it also resembled one of the rocks that surrounded the island. Neither Graham Young, guarding the Goatley at the base of the Hog's Back, nor Freddie Bourne on the bridge of the MTB *344*, was expecting them at that moment. The commando sent to warn them of the team's delay had got lost and only reached the Hog's Back at the same time as the rest of the men.

Nevertheless, and despite the very long delay, Bourne had waited. He had quietly decided to stick around until sunrise if necessary. He wanted no repeat of what had happened only days earlier during Operation Aquatint, when he had to leave commandos behind, including Gus March-Phillips, to be killed and captured by the Germans.

Though the moon made both the MTB and the commandos themselves more visible, it also made their descent down to Pointe Château easier. By 0335hrs they boarded the Goatley and then furiously paddled out to the waiting MTB 344, reaching it in just ten minutes. As they reached the boat, they heard shots being fired after them and stones tumbling down from the cliffs.

The Little Pisser's engines roared as Freddie Bourne steered the boat north towards England. He reported that from the boat they'd not heard the sounds of shooting, but they did hear the engines of another motorboat for about forty-five minutes, and also at a certain point Sark's lighthouse was extinguished. Naturally they were concerned about being discovered, as the MTB was ill prepared for a gunfight with most German ships. Its only advantage was speed. As they sped away from Sark, Lassen recalled, 'the German searchlight lit up the sea. It came from the top of the island, from the old mill, but they were not caught in the beam and after some time it went out.'

The tension of the raid having finally broken, the men spent much of the ride back to Portland cracking jokes and laughing aloud. As Lassen's biographer described the journey back to England:

> When they got well away they started talking. Everybody talked at once and compared what had happened to each. All of a sudden they found out that they had broken international rules by having tied the prisoners' hands and shot them – now that would be something for the German propaganda.

Anders suggested that they should go back and take away the ropes and he looked at Apple seriously. The British talked of the Germans breaking the rules of warfare and now they had done it themselves. The matter was serious and they might get into trouble because of it. If they went back to Sark he was willing to go on land and do the job all alone, he insisted that it should be done. But it was not all as simple as that, on the ship they now had a lot of papers that were of importance for the information office, if they returned to the island now they would risk too much. Apple said that it could not possibly be done so it was no use thinking of it. Sometimes they got orders that did not entirely agree with the international rules and because it was a matter of lives, they had to break them. Those are the difficulties which are above any laws.[23]

As Redborn recalled:

Those orders we received from our superiors were always in accordance with the internationally accepted laws of warfare, but we violated them because our lives were at stake. While we were breaking them, those who framed them were probably fast asleep in their beds. I hope that all who know the truth will understand.[24]

They were now running hours behind schedule, and did not want to be caught in the open sea in daylight. By 0508hrs, a worried naval officer in Portland sent a message to the naval commander in Portsmouth: 'Request air search for JOVIAL be carried out at first light on line Portland Bill to Cape De La Hague.' Jovial was the navy's code name for the raid on Sark. But forty-five minutes later, he became aware of the mission's success and sent out a follow-up cypher message which cancelled the previous message, adding, 'JOVIAL E.T.A. 0630'.

At 0605hrs the men on MTB *344* sighted Portland Bill, the southernmost point of Dorset where a lighthouse is located, and twenty-eight minutes later they entered Portland Harbour. According to one report, they arrived too early at the harbour and needed to wait until the lock was opened. When they finally docked, a lorry took them back to their headquarters at Anderson Manor.

As Lassen remembered it, 'When they got in they had quite a few drinks. The running up and down the Hog's Back had been quite a thirsty job.' But Ian Warren, who was not on the raid, had a slightly different memory. He was sleeping when the commandos returned. Lassen woke him, he recalled. 'He held his unwiped knife under my nose and said: "Look – blood."'[25] In his diary, Lassen wrote: 'Was at it again the other day. The hardest and most difficult job I have ever done – used my knife for the first time.'[26]

Meanwhile, their prisoner, Obergefreiter Hermann Weinreich, was whisked off by MI19 for interrogation at the London Cage. Later that day, Appleyard was summoned to London as well. He had a late afternoon meeting at the Combined Operations Headquarters and met with senior commanders. He also had a private interview with the prime minister in his room in the House of Commons. Churchill personally congratulated him on the success of Operation Basalt, as did General Sir Alan Brooke, the chief of the General Staff. Churchill reportedly growled at Appleyard, saying, 'What have you been up to, my boy?' and put his arm around Appleyard's shoulder.[27]

Appleyard's report, written that day, was endorsed by Mountbatten who presented it to the War Cabinet two days later. Everyone agreed that the raid was a huge success and Appleyard was awarded a Distinguished Service Order while Dudgeon and Lassen were given the Military Cross. Later, he wrote to his brother, using somewhat guarded language:

Last Saturday night really was fun. We spent over four hours there and had a really good browse round before we rang the bell and announced ourselves. It was so strange to see old familiar places again. Such as the tree under which you found half-a-crown! Remember? I recognised it immediately.[28]

In the commando base at Anderson Manor and in London they were celebrating. But on Sark, the Germans were beginning to discover dead bodies.

THE SHOCK OF DISCOVERY

While the commandos were racing to get away from the Dixcart Hotel and back down to their waiting boat, the Germans finally noticed their arrival and began to take countermeasures.

As it turned out later, the Germans had received a report earlier that should have alerted them. In a secret German report following the raid, the commander of the 319th Infantry Division, Major General Müller, reported that at 0210hrs (0110hrs British time):

> Auxiliary Customs Assistant Marburger, who was on guard duty at the pier, heard the distant noise of an engine. By telephone he informed the Orderly Obergefreiter of Number 6 Company of the 583rd Infantry Regiment, Senior Gefreiter Schubert, who did not pass on the information to his Company Commander, who is also the island Commander.

Schubert needed to explain himself, and 'later stated that he waited for confirmation of the report from the strongpoints. He himself did not contact the strongpoints. The interrogation of the strongpoint commanders showed that their guards did not hear any engine noises. Therefore the company commander was not informed and no alarm was given.'[1]

This is a strange report. MTB *344* had cut its engines before the commandos climbed on board the Goatley and paddled to shore several hours before this. The engines were restarted at 0345hrs (0445hrs German time) when they left, on their way back to Portland. At 0210hrs the British boat would have been silent. It is possible that the 'distant noise of an engine' that Marburger heard was not the British raiders at all.

Senior Gefreiter Schubert 'did not pass on the report from the guard at the pier, concerning engine noise, to his company commander', wrote Müller in his report. 'It was his duty to contact the strongpoints concerning the reports of engine noises, and not wait for them to contact him.' Müller therefore decided to court-martial the unfortunate Schubert.[2]

It was not until 0300hrs that Schubert got in touch with Oberleutnant Herdt, the *Inselkommandant*, as it was no longer the possible noise of a boat engine, but the actual sound of shooting that was noticed by those Germans who were awake. It took just five minutes for Herdt to give the order to raise the alarm. At this point the commandos were already on top of the cliff and about to begin their descent to Pointe Château and their waiting boat.

Herdt took personal charge. He ordered the various strongpoints around the island to be alerted. The first of the escaped engineers, Gefreiter Klotz, was discovered, and he was completely naked. He gave an account of what happened and how he had managed to escape from the British soldiers. Herdt ordered Lieutenant Balga to take some men and pursue the commandos as they crossed the Hog's Back. Meanwhile, a customs boat with a crew of five men and carrying a machine gun put out to sea to search for the British boat. Herdt then got through to the regimental command in Guernsey. He told them about the British attack and rushed off to join Balga, who was searching for the commandos. Tracks were found, as well as various objects the commandos had left behind, including two commando knives, a magazine for a sub-machine gun and another for a pistol, a pair of wire cutters, torches, a woollen cap, scarf and several toggle ropes.

The German accounts say nothing about engaging with the commandos, and this is confirmed by the commandos' own reports. Bombardier Redborn later said, 'We could hear the Germans coming after us down the slope.'[3] But, as Tom Keene added, 'Inexplicably, there were no shots, no sounds of pursuit.'[4] The explanation is probably that the Germans had no idea where the commandos had gone. They'd left the Dixcart Hotel and rushed down into the wooded valley. At this point, the most natural direction to take would be straight down to Dixcart Bay, which was a relatively easy walk in either direction. But instead, Appleyard and his men had climbed back up to Petit Dixcart, retracing their route from earlier in the evening. Then they went up on to the Hog's Back and raced down the path to Pointe Château.

By the time Herdt had reached his superiors in Guernsey, the commandos were already at sea, paddling out to the MTB. According to one report, as the boat began to move, 'German searchlights swept the water and machine guns opened up as they sped away from the cliffs of Sark'.[5] This is confirmed by Stokes' account:

> We made it back to the MTB at about 03.45hrs and as we made our escape, the Island was lit by lights and flares and we could now hear the sound of gunfire (not coming in our direction); we made our way safely back to Portland. I think they thought they were being invaded.[6]

As Freddie Bourne took charge of getting the commandos back to England as fast as the Little Pisser could go:

> News of the raid was speeding up the German chain of command: Division HQ was notified at 3.50 a.m.; LXXXIV Corps HQ at 4.30 a.m., and Seventh Army HQ at 6.10 a.m.

At 6.45 a.m. the news had reached Army Group D in Paris and the Chief of the General Staff. Within three hours an eleven-point questionnaire was telephoned from Ob. West.[7]

Even before the commandos made it back to Portland, the first repercussions of the raid were being felt on Sark. At 0400hrs a German soldier pounded at the door of the Dixcart Hotel, awakening Miss Duckett and Miss Page, the joint managers of the hotel. They were accused of hiding British soldiers, which they denied. They insisted that they'd slept throughout the raid, though it took place, including the firefight, only a few metres away from their bedroom. According to one report, 'The two ladies sat up for the rest of the night drinking mint tea, interrupted from time to time by more Germans who simply would not believe their story that they knew nothing about the Commando raid.'[8] They later claimed that until they saw two German coffins the following morning, they had no idea the British had attacked. The Germans didn't believe them and ransacked the hotel as they searched for evidence of British commandos in hiding.

Meanwhile, the Dame of Sark was told about the raid by the Germans. They demanded that islanders evacuate a number of buildings in the centre of the island from noon that day. She was later sent a message demanding that her two-horse van be sent to the Dixcart Hotel. It turned out that the van was needed to transport coffins down to Creux Harbour. There were two coffins, marked with swastikas and draped with German flags. This was almost certainly because the Germans didn't immediately find Oswald's body, though some islanders have speculated that two bodies were taken off the island in one of the coffins.

Julia Tremayne's home was within a few metres of the Dixcart Hotel and she certainly would have heard the shots and the commotion. She wrote about the raid in her secret letters:

There has actually been an invasion landing on Sark but so little is allowed to be known yet and the crop of rumours is just amazing. I reckon you will know by the wireless and get a more correct account than we have here. Last night after a very hot day, a thick fog came up and blotted out the Islands, at about 4 AM. There was an awful noise, machine-gunning etc, and some say a boat landed in Dixcart Bay with twenty of our men. This we do know, a lot of German wounded have been seen and one or two Germans have been taken away and some killed. I know this for certain, for last evening when I was going to church I walked behind a cart with the coffins, covered with a swastika flag. Yesterday the German troops got so frightened that the whole lot cleared out of Stock's Hotel and went down to sleep in the girl's school. All carts were commandeered to take every bed and divan from the hotel. The schoolroom furniture and all Miss Howard's school house furniture was thrown into the playground and later stored in the little prison. It was such an upheaval on God's day. They are terror-stricken and I think want to hide behind the civilians and be nearer the harbour for getting away if things get too hot for them.

Poor Mrs Rondel and Elizabeth have had orders to leave their house at a few hours' notice. We have offered them part of this house, but no one is safe. Any day the order may come for us to leave and go to Germany. There are still more heartaches now, for the Manoir and all its cottages have had three hours' notice to clear out. All the troops are leaving their billets on the coast and massing inland, so these poor souls have had to scatter all over the island. Some have lived in their houses for fifty years. The Gestapo are still here, questioning everybody about the landing of the British. It has proved uncertain how many there were, some say ten or more now, and they must have known the place well, for it is so heavily mined and barbed wired. I am glad none of our soldiers were captured. The order for so many to leave their homes is a form of punishment, I suppose. The curfew is now from 8.30

till 7 am. Also we hear Mr Isaac Carré has been taken off the Island, his son is in the Merchant Service, so perhaps they think he may have been one, but it is hard luck that the father has been captured. On the night of the raid Mr and Mrs Falle were awakened in the middle of the night by two Germans at the bedside with fixed bayonets looking for any likely intruders. It is hard to believe we are only eighty miles from Weymouth, the fog is very thick and has been for days, but when it clears I should look to see the Islands surrounded by the English and American fleets! I never thought our men would land here, it was a plucky, daring attempt. The German news says it was an outrage and that the Germans were murdered in their beds and those taken prisoner were bound and taken away in their shirts and not allowed to dress. Of course, we don't believe it. Poor little Sark must be well in the limelight if accounts are true, and I am sure you must be very worried about us, perhaps you are thinking we have been shipped off to Germany by this time. Eleven only went from Sark and our turn is not yet. Please God it won't come.[9]

THE CARPENTER SINGS

As the Little Pisser raced back to the safety of Portland Harbour, the commandos radioed back a previously agreed code. It was 'A-1-0'. This meant the operation was successful, one prisoner had been captured and there were no casualties on the British side.

As Captain Colin Ogden-Smith wrote in his diary, summarising the raid: 'Spent 4½ hours ashore after stiff cliff climbs. Found 5 Jerrys, brought 1 back. Had very interesting interview with an inhabitant. All returned safely.'[1] From their point of view, the raid was an unqualified success. But the events that followed had wide ranging implications and would cause some to conclude that Operation Basalt had been a failure. It is only by looking over all the consequences of the raid that one can decide if it was a success.

It may be useful, therefore, to start with the interrogation of the prisoner, which was the whole point of the raid in the first place, and to explore the German reaction to the raid, which has been the focus of much attention by historians, with Hitler's infamous 'Commando Order' getting the most attention. But these were not the only consequences of Operation Basalt. For thousands of prisoners, both German and Allied, the raid on Sark was followed by tit-for-tat retaliations. That was part of a massive German propaganda campaign which aimed to depict the commandos as 'terrorists'. But while accusing the

British of criminal behaviour, the German command then carried out a series of punitive deportations of innocent Channel Islanders, including a large group from Sark, which was clearly a breach of international law and a war crime.

In purely military terms the raid also had consequences, as the German occupiers were forced to beef up their defences on Sark, to commit more troops to the island and to lay thousands more mines. As Alan and Mary Wood wrote in their 1955 book *Islands in Danger*:

> There is no doubt about what was accomplished by Appleyard and his men. The thousands of mines round Sark and the other islands could have been used against Allied soldiers when the landing came in Normandy. Every gun on the island was a gun wasted for Hitler; every soldier meant one man less for other fronts.

They quote General Walter Warlimont, deputy chief of the German Armed Forces Operations Staff, who wrote immediately after the Sark raid that 'nowhere can be considered safe. The enemy may strike at any time and any place.'[2]

All of the consequences need to be weighed up in order to determine whether Operation Basalt was a success as Appleyard first believed when he radioed 'A-1-0' on the way home that night. Within hours of the commandos' return to Portland, the question of whether Operation Basalt had been worth it was answered, and answered definitively. The entire purpose of the raid had been to capture a live German prisoner and interrogate him, and that had been achieved.

Getting hold of live German prisoners in 1942 was not easy in that part of the world. The last British troops had withdrawn from France in 1940 and German forces were safely ensconced behind the Atlantic Wall while the Allies made their preparations for an eventual invasion of north-western Europe. It was vital to learn all that was possible about Nazi-occupied Europe, and there was no better way than to capture and interrogate

German prisoners – ideally, German soldiers who knew something about the defences in place. Had the prisoner yielded no useful intelligence, the raid would still have been a success, but as it turned out, the intelligence that was collected proved to be immensely useful.

As soon as the Little Pisser arrived in Portland and the commandos disembarked, they turned over their prisoner to MI19. Later accounts agreed that the prisoner, Obergefreiter Hermann Weinreich, proved a very useful source of information. Major Appleyard wrote to his brother in guarded language not long after the raid:

> Our enforced guest of the evening has proved to be a winner! And I saw a report yesterday saying that he was considered to be the most useful prisoner obtained by anyone up to date. He has proved very chatty and nothing is too much trouble for him to describe in detail.[3]

As Appleyard's father later wrote:

> The prisoner obtained on this raid supplied all the information that was required, and the great importance that was attached to the operation as a whole can be gathered from the last few paragraphs of Geoff's own letter in which he describes meeting the Prime Minister and other War Chiefs on the following day.[4]

MI19 took Obergefreiter Weinreich to a mansion in Kensington Palace Gardens known as the 'London Cage'. This is where German prisoners were interrogated. It later morphed into the War Crimes Investigation Unit when it became clearer that prisoners were yielding important information that would prove useful for any post-war trials.

The commander of the Cage was a 60-something lieutenant colonel named A.P. Scotland, who came out of retirement to run the interrogation of German prisoners. In his book written a decade after the war ended, Scotland included a photograph that was captioned, 'British intelligence officers conduct a demonstration in the technique of interrogating the prisoner.' It showed two British soldiers sitting behind a table as a 'German prisoner' stood at attention some distance away, facing them. There is some evidence that interrogations in the Cage were not always so formal, and after the war there were allegations of torture.

While much of the intelligence collected from German prisoners consisted of things that could be filed away for later use, sometimes the information was of immediate relevance. According to a report of the first interrogation of Weinreich, just hours after his capture by the commandos, the former carpenter reported that 'the work he was carrying out on the old harbour is the fixing of a boom defence across the entrance … This work had not been completed by the time he left and he does not know what additional strengthening will take place.'[5] The work hadn't been completed, according to Weinreich, because of 'lack of materials', and he told his British interrogators that a ship carrying those materials from Guernsey to Sark would arrive on Tuesday, 6 October, between 0930 and 1000hrs. This was two days after the commando raid.

As the MI19 officers noted in their report, 'This information was passed to the Admiralty, 2330 hours, 4 Oct 42.' This was less than twenty-four hours after the raid on Sark. Whether the Admiralty acted on the information is not known, but this was the kind of precise, real-time intelligence that could prove immeasurably useful. And it was just the tip of the iceberg.

Weinreich had been in Sark for just a couple of weeks, previously having been based in Guernsey and before that in France. As an engineer, his field of expertise was the network of defences that constituted the Atlantic Wall. This was precisely the kind of information that the Allies needed. It was only by chance that the commandos had stumbled upon a group of sleeping engineers. They could just as easily have captured the customs officials patrolling the island, or even cooks or other support personnel. To have captured engineers was pure luck.

MI19 asked Weinreich if the Germans had mined the beaches on Sark, as the commandos had assumed. He replied that:

> He has never heard of minefields being used on the beaches, and replied that the salt water would render them useless. Minefields are clearly identified by being surrounded by barbed wire and having a notice on each side – Achtung Minen. P/W states that Tellerminen are laid at a greater depth than S-mines. [Teller mines were German anti-tank mines.]

Weinreich's comments about the 'bouncing Betties' (S-mines) may not have been entirely truthful. While certain kinds of mines could not be exposed to salt water, they could be placed in close proximity to the beach, for example, just above the high-water mark. The occasional discovery of mines in and around Sark's beaches continued for many decades after the war. The British interrogators also wanted to know about mines in the sea around the Channel Islands. Weinreich said he didn't think they existed, 'as fishing boats go in and out quite freely and unescorted.'

Weinreich's interrogation continued for several days and as an engineer he could speak authoritatively about German defences along the entire Atlantic Wall. This information would prove useful not only in future small-scale raids, but also when the time came to land hundreds of thousands of Allied troops in France. His particular expertise seemed to be mines. He explained:

> The mines are laid out in rows in such a fashion that every mine is five paces away from its neighbour, either vertically or diagonally. S-mines are laid just deep enough to be covered by soil, with the contact pins sticking out of the ground. The mine is exploded either by kicking against the contact pin or treading on it. The mine contains a safety device consisting of a piece of

metal about one inch long and two millimetres in diameter. It is screwed out of the mine when it is laid. To re-secure the mine it is sufficient to insert some metal object, e.g., a nail, which will fit into the hole and thus make a closure of the circuit impossible.

Weinreich told MI19 that he had 'never seen any evidence of bridges or roads being mined. He has no knowledge of booby-traps, anti-lifting devices or trip wires.'

The British were keen to know as much as possible about defences on Sark – information that would prove useful for future raids there and on other Channel Islands. Weinreich's account is incredibly detailed:

The approach from the harbour to the G.P.O. [General Post Office] is barred in two places by barbed wire, which runs at right-angles to the road. The road itself is barricaded with a knife rest about 4 metres long. The barricade on either side of the road consists of double apron wire, reinforced with concertina entanglements. It is estimated that the first of these barricades occurs about 750 yards from the harbour. The barbed wire used is the ordinary type. P/W was unable to give any other details or locations, but he affirms that there is no wire in the hamlet.

Weinreich believed that there were between 200 and 300 German troops on Sark, plus another twenty or thirty artillerymen, though he didn't see any big guns. He was certain that the artillerymen he saw were 'army artillery, wearing field grey, with the usual red piping'.

A week after the raid, Weinreich continued to provide useful intelligence.[6] He admitted that he'd not been around the island very much in the few days he was based there, but said he saw no road blocks in the hamlet or anywhere else. He also had no knowledge of passwords that were being used there. He said there were no road signs on the island, which made sense as Sark had no motor vehicles before the Germans arrived. His knowledge of the island's fortifications was fairly limited, though in his opinion there were 'more than two strong points on Sark'.

More than a week after the raid, the British were still analysing the information that had been collected from Weinreich, as well as captured documents, including pay books. The latter 'provided some useful Order of Battle Information', they wrote. But MI19 were not entirely happy with the information he provided. Weinreich, they wrote, 'was an unreliable witness and contradicted himself in two important respects … His information can therefore, at the most, only be taken as conclusive for those localities in which he himself was stationed, i.e. Guernsey and Sark.'

THE PROPAGANDA WAR BEGINS

While British interrogators were questioning Obergefreiter Weinreich, his comrades on Sark were shocked at the discovery of precisely what had happened in the early hours of the morning on 4 October 1942. Not only had a German soldier been captured, but it turned out that several of the engineers had their hands tied. Two of them were shot and killed with their hands still bound.

The Nazi propaganda machine went into overdrive, as Reich Minister of Propaganda Joseph Goebbels never missed an opportunity to accuse the Allies of war crimes. This may be hard to imagine now, but during the war the Nazi regime was desperate to win the support of public opinion not only in the neutral countries, but even in Britain. Though Nazis are now always portrayed as being simply evil and not at all concerned with how they appeared to others, during the war their propaganda, which was often quite sophisticated and nuanced, sought to show their enemies as being the ones carrying out war crimes.

On the day after the raid, according to one account:

Berlin Radio broadcast an announcement signed by Dr Goebbels: 'Sixteen British fell upon a German working party … whom they tied up in their shirts with a thin but strong cord. The men were not allowed to put on more clothes … When they resisted this improper treatment they were killed by bullets and bayonets.'[1]

The Nazis were eager to show that the tying of prisoners' hands was part of a pattern of inhumane behaviour by British commandos. They were particularly interested in demonstrating a link between what the commandos had done on Sark and a leaflet recovered from Allied soldiers captured in the Dieppe raid six weeks earlier. That leaflet showed ways to restrain prisoners, and the Germans insisted that the Allies had a policy of shackling captured soldiers.

In addition to the traditional Nazi propaganda organs, the Germans had use of the censored newspapers on the occupied Channel Islands to get their message out. On the front page of *The Star* ('Guernsey's Oldest Newspaper') on Thursday, 8 October, there were the usual reports of the Wehrmacht 'tightening its grip on Stalingrad' and 'misbehaviour' by British and American troops in Iceland. It contained long quotes from 'Lord Haw-Haw', the Irish-American Nazi propagandist William Joyce, who was hanged for treason after the war. Joyce wrote about the failure of the Western powers to open a second front. All this was standard fare in the Nazi-controlled press.

But nearly halfway down the front page of the newspaper there was a article headlined 'British attack and bind German troops in Sark – Immediate Reprisals for Disgraceful Episode'. The article went on at length, with quotes from the German Supreme Command laying out what they discovered after the raiders left, and ending with this chilling message:

> In future all terrorist and sabotage parties of the British and their confederates, who do not act like soldiers but like bandits, will be treated by the German troops as such, and wherever they are encountered they will be *ruthlessly wiped out in action.*[2]

The *Guernsey Evening Press*, another well-established Channel Islands newspaper now under Nazi control, continued with its version of the story as dictated by the German occupiers, on the following day. Though there were also stories about an interview granted by Field Marshal Rommel to journalists in Berlin and a story optimistically titled 'Encircled Soviets Wiped Out', the main story was 'British Raid on Sark – How Germany Views Futile Attempt'. This article relied on a radio broadcast from Edward Roderick Deedsoe from Bremen which condemned the 'unsoldierly' behaviour of the British commandos. Deedsoe was furious:

> German soldiers had been surrounded, and it did not matter whether the order came from a highly placed officer or from an N.C.O. [non-commissioned officer], German soldiers had their hands bound in deplorable and outrageous fashion. All this tended to show to what extent the traditions of the British Army were being modernised so that men, yelled at through loud-speakers, and taught how to make bayonet thrusts at an enemy under conditions that might be compared to Chicago gangsterism, could have a chance to put such lessons into practice – in Sark!

He added that:

> [The] German High Command had never found it necessary to resort to such instruction of the baser instincts, but relied rather on the chivalry of the German soldier to do his duty in warfare ... Perhaps this form of raid arises from the sense of frustration on the part of, I hope, individual soldiers. Perhaps it springs from a loss of temper and the hopelessness of defeating the enemy that such resort to forms of humiliating the enemy is made. But it is most degrading to the British Army, not to the German soldier, that such things have been allowed to happen.

Deedsoe said that, as for the German people, 'their morale was not weakened' by such raids, 'indeed, were they strengthened in their firm resolve not to throw up the sponge, but to grit their teeth and say that to win the war was the only way of gaining possession in full of what was their due'.[3]

Note how the wording of Deedsoe's article is designed to appeal to an English-speaking audience. It speaks of the 'traditions of the British Army' in a positive way, even if today they behaved like 'Chicago gangsters'. And it made suggestions that the British were simply suffering from 'the hopelessness of defeating' the Wehrmacht, but perhaps at heart remained decent men. This language aimed to influence public opinion, primarily in England, and in particular to strengthen those in Britain who were still advocating an agreement with the Germans to end the war.

In the next few days, the British Government tried to cope with the German propaganda by telling its side of the story:

> The raid on Sark was carried out by a party of 10 officers and men. Seven of the party captured five Germans. The hands of the Germans were tied in order that arms might be linked with the captors. No orders – written or otherwise, had been issued. But the prisoners had to be taken past a German-occupied barracks on the way to the boats, and precautions were therefore necessary. In spite of the precautions, four of the five German prisoners of war broke away, shouting, and had to be shot to prevent them raising the alarm.[4]

It is interesting that the War Cabinet statement gets the number of raiders wrong (ten instead of twelve) and specifically cites the number of seven capturing the Germans. Revealing the precise number of men involved in capturing the Germans may have been done to highlight just how few the commandos were, and how evenly matched they were with their German prisoners. But it does raise the question about the missing three men.

On 9 October, the *Daily Telegraph* answered the German charges by noting that:

> There is nothing in the Geneva Convention of 1921, which Britain and Germany both signed, against the tying up of captives in the process of catching them – the rules do not deal with conditions during action or in circumstances where it might be essential to prevent a prisoner from being a source of danger.[5]

Even nine days after the raid, coverage of it continued to dominate the front pages of the occupied Channel Island newspapers. *The Star* gave nearly half a page to a summary of Lord Haw-Haw's broadcast from the previous afternoon. 'The most unsuccessful war-lord of all times, Winston Churchill, tries to take his revenge by binding German prisoners,' he said. 'He is binding England as well, and to a mill-stone which is dragging her down.'[6]

He contrasted Hitler's caution in risking the lives of German soldiers, preferring to rely on air power and artillery, to the British contempt for human life as shown by their treatment of prisoners of war. He reviewed British statements on the Sark raid and the earlier raid on Dieppe and concluded: 'Now instead of offering the apology which is due for the behaviour of British and associated troops concerning the treatment of German prisoners, the British government takes refuge in flimsy excuses, equivocations, evasions and, in particular, the argument that humanity varies according to circumstances.'

He contrasted this with the 'chivalrous' Wehrmacht:

> The German Supreme Command have never deemed it necessary to resort to such distinction. They have observed a standard of chivalry in which the British Government evidently does not believe. In the German view, the binding of prisoners of war is a barbarous and unconscionable practice admitting of no excuses.
>
> The British Government also argues that prisoners of war may be bound because the Geneva Convention does not forbid binding. The Geneva Convention does not forbid the

use, either, of thumb-screws or the rack, for the same reason – namely, that those who framed it did not consider such a prohibition to be necessary … Moreover it is impossible to believe that the British troops on Sark had no orders, written or otherwise. The only answer to these tactics and persistence in outrage lies in reprisals such as have been announced by the German Supreme Command.[7]

Several of the German accounts dismissed the British claims that the prisoners had had their hands tied in order to allow the commandos to take them down safely to the waiting Goatley. One German propagandist argued that the trail on the Hog's Back did not allow men to walk side by side, they'd need to walk single file, so there was really no excuse for the tying of hands. But the British were not claiming the prisoners would walk three or four abreast on the narrow trail; instead the idea had been to attach each prisoner to a commando for the walk down.

The points the Germans scored with this early propaganda continued to resonate even after the war. In his 1946 history of the occupation of the Channel Islands, British historian Durand wrote that the Germans:

… argued that the British statement afforded proof that a British military order for the 'chaining' [sic] of German prisoners actually existed; it scored a point by remarking that the shooting of the prisoners must have made a greater noise than could be made by escaping men trying to raise an alarm; and it denied that the prisoners on their way to the boat had to pass barracks occupied by German troops.

But Durand countered that last point, writing:

It could be that the rifle shots would have made more actual noise than could be made by an escaping prisoner but they may have escaped notice before daybreak in an island patrolled by nervous sentries, whereas an escaped prisoner who dashed into quarters occupied by Germans clad only in his shirt and shouting for help could hardly fail to attract attention.[8]

While the shooting would have awakened the sleeping Germans on the island, letting one of the captives get away would have been far more dangerous. An escaped prisoner could have told his comrades how many commandos had landed, where they had come from and where they were going.

There was much that the German propagandists left out or got wrong, such as failing to mention that all five captured soldiers had to be awakened, sometimes with great difficulty, by the commandos. They also referred to the use of bayonets, not realising that the commandos – in this case, Lassen – were using a very special knife.

Neither the Germans in their propaganda, nor Major Appleyard in his reports and even his letters home, mentioned Lassen's killing of the sentry, Peter Oswald. The Germans were probably embarrassed by his failure to raise the alarm. And the British, including Appleyard in his private correspondence, may not have wished to highlight the often brutal and very personal nature of commando fighting.

The German propaganda onslaught was only the beginning. Hitler was furious and far worse was to come.

THE WEHRMACHT TAKES MEASURES

While Berlin and London were busy with the propaganda war, on the Channel Islands in general and on Sark in particular, the German occupation forces were taking steps to ensure that there would be no repeat of Operation Basalt.

Generalfeldmarschall Gerd von Rundstedt, commander-in-chief in the west, 'pointed out angrily that the raid had succeeded only because orders had been disobeyed'.[1] In particular, he was furious that the order to billet German soldiers far from the vulnerable clifftops of Sark and to keep them concentrated around the centre of the island had been ignored.

As mentioned earlier, on the morning following the raid, German officers came to speak with the Dame of Sark:

Mrs Hathaway was informed that the Germans were taking over an area of land in the centre of Sark – the Junior School and every small cottage and building nearby were summarily requisitioned. Evacuation, removal of all household belongings and furnishings had to be completed by noon. The Germans were already laying fresh barbed wire entanglements and siting machine-guns for this new 'hedgehog' strongpoint – [Major General] Müller [the commander of all German forces in the

Channel Islands] had ordered that all German troops should be housed within the perimeter.[2]

It was decided to turn Sark into a full-scale *Festung* (fortress), and initially cliffs and beaches were closed to the local inhabitants. Curfews were now tightened and ran from 10 p.m. to 9 a.m. Dogs running loose were shot by soldiers on patrol.

Thousands of mines were sown on the cliffs and on some of the very best pasture land. By the end of the war, Sark had some 13,000 German mines – more than two dozen for every inhabitant of the island. These mines not only cut into the land that locals could use for farming and severely restricted their access to the coast, but inevitably caused tragedy. On 3 October 1944, the second anniversary of Operation Basalt, a 4-year-old girl, Nanette Hamon, died after straying into one of the German minefields near her home.

The islanders noticed the changes to the German defences. Julia Tremayne wrote in one of her secret letters: 'No guns have been erected on the church tower but all church windows looking on the German quarters have been bricked up with red bricks. The Germans are terrified that our men will land again and take pot-shots at them.'[3]

Armoured vehicles were brought over to the island, including two guns on Renault chassis, brought over from Guernsey. (They were eventually returned to the larger island.) It is not clear if more soldiers were sent to Sark. According to British reports, 'Air photographs do NOT show any increase in military activity.'[4]

Within hours of the raid having taken place, the Geheime Feldpolizei (sometimes confused with the Gestapo) arrived to interrogate locals and investigate the army as well. Oberleutnant Heinz Herdt, the *Inselkommandant*, was responsible for what had happened on the night of 3–4 October. There are conflicting reports about his fate. According to several sources, Major General Müller ordered a court martial for Herdt and relieved him of his post for 'not taking strict precautions against raiders and for allowing men to sleep in undefended billets. The Germans in the Channel Islands now realised for the first time that they were in the front line.'[5] Decades after the war, local historian Richard Heaume wrote: 'As a result [of the commando raid], Herdt was court-martialled for failing to protect a billet of the Engineer Detachment in the company reserve'.[6] But Herdt's daughter, Doris Theuerkauf, disputes this. 'As far as I know,' she writes, 'my father was not court-martialled, but there was a research by the military justice.'[7]

Just four days after the raid, Herdt was replaced by Lieutenant Knauf, who held the post temporarily, and Herdt returned to Guernsey. But nine months later, Herdt was back in Sark, again as *Inselkommandant*. Why he was never punished for the failure at the time of the commando raid is unclear. There is some speculation that this may have been due to the influence of the Dame of Sark, who had very good connections with the German command in Guernsey and who liked Herdt.[8]

The effects of the raid on Sark were felt throughout the Channel Islands. On Guernsey, the German forces stepped up their vigilance. They patrolled the main roads and the coast throughout the night. Roads were barricaded to the great inconvenience of locals, who could not reach their workplaces until late morning as a result. The decision to regroup the soldiers into easily defensible positions was applied on Guernsey as it was on Sark. Many locals were evicted from their homes, including some bedridden invalids.

The German reaction to Operation Basalt, with its panicked shipping of unnecessary armour to Sark, the placement of thousands of landmines, the imposition of a curfew and the redeployment of German forces to more secure parts of the island – and the fact that this was repeated on other islands – confirms the success of the mission.

The German occupation forces throughout the Channel Islands had been spooked.

17

A WAR CRIME IS REVEALED

If the capture and interrogation of Obergefreiter Weinreich, more than anything else, demonstrated the success of the raid, it was the intelligence collected from Mrs Frances Pittard that may have had the greatest impact. Based on what she told Major Appleyard, and the Guernsey newspapers she gave to him, the world learned for the first time of the war crimes being carried out by the German occupation forces on British soil. Until the commandos returned home with this information early on the morning of 4 October 1942, no one in Britain was aware of Hitler's orders to deport 2,000 British subjects, all of them civilians, from the Channel Islands to camps in Germany.

Three days after the raid, an internal memorandum circulated in London began with the words: 'This very successful operation has provided invaluable intelligence.' It then went into some detail, not all of it accurate, about what had been learned about the deportations. Some of Mrs Pittard's information was also confirmed by Obergefreiter Weinreich:

According to the prisoner of war and supported by para. 2. of a proclamation in a captured copy of the GUERNSEY 'Star and Evening Express' signed 'Knackfuss, Oberst. *Feldkommandant*', all male civilians – (i) not born in the Channel Islands; (ii) not permanently resident there – between the ages of 16 and 60, have been deported to Germany together with their families, for forced labour.

This deportation took place last week at the shortest notice and 900 men were conscripted from GUERNSEY, 400 are still to go and it is expected that there will be more from JERSEY than from GUERNSEY. The only exceptions were clergymen, doctors, fishermen and men working in the harbours. Warm clothing, etc. was collected from the remaining Islanders.

Eleven men of SARK were warned to be ready to go last week. Two committed suicide and only nine left. The SARK men are believed to have gone, not to Germany but to TOURAINE in France.

It is considered that the above intelligence should be brought to the notice of the Foreign Office and P.W.E.

The raid had discovered information that could be used by the Foreign Office and the Political Warfare Executive (PWE), a clandestine body closely linked to the SOE. But it was never the intention of the British Government to publicly reveal what its commandos learned on any of these raids.

However, two things about this raid were different. First, the unexpected news about the deportation of innocent British civilians to Germany was a major war crime and could be used by the Allies. And second, the Germans themselves gave out a great deal of information about the raid, including operational details, much of it untrue, and this needed to be countered.

The Churchill government was not keen to raise the issue of how the Germans were behaving on the Channel Islands at any point in the war, in part because it would raise the question of why the British Government was not doing more to help the islanders, or even why the Channel Islands had been abandoned in the first place. The islanders on Sark and elsewhere did feel neglected and forgotten. Even Mrs Pittard had asked the commandos during their short visit why the king had failed to mention the islands in his Christmas speech.

Once the news about the deportations reached London, the government felt under pressure to do something, not least from the Channel Islanders who had been evacuated to England in 1940. The British needed to tell their side of the story of the raid and this included revealing the truth about the deportations of Channel Islanders to camps in Germany. As Madeleine Bunting put it in her book, *The Model Occupation*:

> *The Times, Daily Sketch* and *Daily Mirror* devoted considerable space to this latest instance of German barbarity. Headlines ran 'Nazis Send Captured Britons as Slaves, Island Raid Reveals' and 'Islanders Starve as Nazis Grab Food'. Under the title 'It Might Have Been Your Fate' the *Sunday Chronicle* declared that Oberst Knackfuss, the *Feldkommandant*, 'should go down on the black list alongside the murderers of Lidice and those who stole the food from the Greeks and left them to starve … the real truth has emerged of deportations and forced labour'.[1]

A month after the raid in November 1942, the London-based Channel Islands Refugee Committee published a twenty-eight-page pamphlet entitled 'Conditions in Guernsey – as revealed in certain issues of the Guernsey "Evening Press" and Guernsey "Star" between September 16th and October 2nd, 1942'. It opened with this sentence: 'A few issues of the *Guernsey Star* and *Evening Press* have recently arrived in this country.'[2] But it didn't explain how they arrived – from Mrs Pittard's home via the commandos.

As people in Britain began to learn about the deportations that had taken place, some contacted government ministries in the hope of learning more details. A poignant example came just two weeks after the raid in a letter from Mr R.A. Skelton who wrote to the commander of the London Cage, Lieutenant Colonel Scotland:

I have been in communication with the Admiralty to ascertain if possible whether my brother, Major J.H. Skelton, who has been in Sark (an interrupted visit) since June 1940, is among the 9 men deported from the island last month. It occurred to me that your raiding party will almost certainly have brought back some information as to the names of these few men. As you will well understand, I should be grateful for any information relevant to my brother.

It is not clear if Scotland was able to tell Mr Skelton that his brother had taken his own life rather than accept deportation to Germany.

The revelation of the German mistreatment of British subjects in the Channel Islands probably contributed to a stiffening of resolve in Britain at a critical moment in the war. And according to Bunting, 'the government was deeply troubled, and within a few months the deportations had been quietly listed as a war crime, for which the Germans could be prosecuted after the war'.[3]

'*Could* be prosecuted' – but in fact, no one ever was.

18

TIT FOR TAT

The German response to Operation Basalt, and in particular the binding of the hands of captured soldiers by the commandos, repeatedly referred to Dieppe. On 19 August 1942, little more than six weeks before the Sark raid, the Allies had landed troops at the French port of Dieppe. The aim of that raid, which involved several thousand troops including commandos from the Canadian, British and American armies, aimed to capture the port and test German defences. After just a few hours, the Allies were forced to withdraw, the majority of the men who made it ashore having been killed, wounded or captured.

According to an internal British memo, 'The German High Command declared that the men [on Sark] had been illegitimately roped and that it was while resisting this that two had been shot, and treated this alleged barbarity as a sequel to similar alleged barbarity at Dieppe'. The British did eventually concede that there had been 'an unauthorised order at Dieppe to tie the hands of prisoners to prevent them from destroying papers. The order had been countermanded, and in fact none of the Dieppe prisoners had had their hands tied.'[1]

None of the Germans taken prisoner at Dieppe had their hands tied – which may explain why the 'alleged barbarity at Dieppe' did not provoke the kind of fierce reaction that the Sark raid did. But, the memo continued, it was not only in Dieppe that the British had committed this kind of war crime:

In the midst of a storm of libellous allegations against the Allies – extending from the employment of prisoners to clear mines in the Mediterranean, and the shooting of shipwrecked soldiers in the Levant, through the gagging and binding of a German prisoner taken on the Lofoten Islands and the machine-gunning of some first aid units of the Folgare Division, besides other Libyan atrocities, down to keeping Japanese in prisoners of war camps on the cold ground – they announced the shackling of all officers and men taken at Dieppe.[2]

A total of 1,376 British prisoners were to be shackled in reprisal not only for the raid on Sark, but for all the alleged British atrocities carried out so far. The behaviour of the commandos on Sark was the final straw.

The British response to the shackling of Allied prisoners was to have Combined Operations Headquarters publish an account of the raid:

Adding certain details as to the forced deportation of the inhabitants of Sark … A number of points were now brought into controversy, such as how far a distinction could be drawn between what may be done in the course of battle and what may be done after the prisoner is in safe custody, and whether there were any barracks on the island.

The Germans had responded to a spurious war crime committed by the British with a genuine one of their own. As the official historian of the occupied Channel Islands, Charles Cruickshank writes:

In Sark the prisoners had been bound merely so that their arms would be linked with those of their captors. When they escaped they had to be shot to prevent them from raising the alarm. The Geneva Convention said nothing about tying prisoners, but merely prescribed humane treatment. The Convention did forbid reprisals, however, and the German government was clearly guilty.[3]

As Brian Lett put it, 'The Geneva Convention simply did not contemplate the situation in which the SSRF had found itself.'[4]

In addition to rebutting German charges of inhumane behaviour, the Canadian Government then announced that it would shackle an equal number of German prisoners. The prisoners of war who were shackled did not always meekly accept their new treatment. In a prisoner-of-war camp in Bowmanville, Ontario, a decision was made to shackle over 100 German prisoners. The prisoners rebelled, engaging in hand-to-hand fighting with their guards in what has come to be known as the 'Battle of Bowmanville' and which lasted for a couple of days. As *Time* magazine put it at the time, 'When the Canadians came with the manacles, the big blond Nazi boys at Camp Bowmanville put up an awful fight.'[5] The Germans were eventually subdued with tear gas and fire hoses.

The German prisoners in Canada had their chains removed two months later following a proposal by the Swiss Government. The Germans hesitated to do the same with their shackled prisoners, demanding that in addition the British Government needed to give an assurance that they would no longer engage in the shackling of captured German soldiers. They were eventually satisfied that this was the case.

Though the British made a strong case that the Geneva Convention did not forbid the temporary tying of hands of captured soldiers under battlefield conditions, behind the scenes there was a debate in Cabinet and there was concern that, legal or not, the binding of prisoners was not helpful. On future raids, the commandos had clear orders not to repeat this.

Lord Louis Mountbatten, chief of Combined Operations, distanced himself from what the commandos had done on Sark. In a letter, he wrote:

I specifically told Major Appleyard (if my memory serves me right) before he undertook the raid on Sark that he was not to tie the hands of any of his prisoners. Unfortunately this order was disregarded … One of the prisoners gave out a great cry for help and ran away in the dark. The Commandos shot him as he ran. The others were brought back to safety with their hands bound. Their hands were immediately untied when they got into the boat.[6]

Mountbatten's memory clearly failed him on at least one point, as only one prisoner was taken alive. Perhaps his recollection of Appleyard's 'disregarding' of his order was also inaccurate. In any event, Appleyard never had the chance to respond to his commander's allegation.

19

THE COMMANDO ORDER

As with any military operation, there were short-term and long-term effects of Operation Basalt. We've already seen some of the results of the raid, including the successful interrogation of a prisoner and the revelations about German war crimes which came courtesy of Mrs Pittard and the newspapers she gave to the commandos. Many of the effects were predictable and typically followed every raid of this kind, such as disciplinary measures against the *Inselkommandant* and decisions to tighten security on the island. And there were some dramatic repercussions as well, including the temporary shackling of thousands of prisoners, both Allied and German, for many weeks after the raid.

But the most significant result of Operation Basalt was surely the infamous 'Commando Order' (*Kommandobefehl*), issued by Hitler himself on 18 October 1942, exactly two weeks after the raid on Sark (see the full text in Appendix 2). The order was a continuation of previous measures announced, including the shackling of the Dieppe prisoners, which followed that raid, but it also went beyond those measures.[1]

The order was marked 'secret' and was limited in its distribution to just twelve copies. To make certain that the Wehrmacht heads were aware of just how sensitive the order was, each copy contained these sentences: 'This order is intended for Commanders only and is in no circumstances to fall into

Enemy hands. Further distribution by receiving Headquarters is to be most strictly limited.'

The order, which was later recognised as a war crime, ironically began by raising the issue of international law – 'For a long time now our opponents have been employing in their conduct of the war, methods which contravene the International Convention of Geneva.' This is an extraordinary statement and expresses a bizarre Nazi obsession (in their propaganda) with international law and Geneva Conventions at a time when they were inventing new *categories* of war crimes and crimes against humanity, especially on the Eastern Front.

It was not the only time the Nazis would raise issues of international law and accuse their enemies of violations. They justified the deportations of innocent civilians from Sark and the other Channel Islands in September 1942 because of what the British had done in Iran a year earlier. They routinely referred to the Royal Air Force's Bomber Command as war criminals, most notably following the bombing of Dresden in February 1945. Goebbels' propaganda was particularly effective in that case, and his wildly inflated casualty figures and characterisation of Dresden as a 'city of culture' with no military value was widely accepted long after the Nazi regime disappeared.

In the October 1942 Commando Order, Hitler's description of the British raiding party on Sark reads almost like a description of his own elite forces, especially the SS:

> The members of the so-called Commandos behave in a particularly brutal and underhand manner; and it has been established that those units recruit criminals not only from their own country but even former convicts set free in enemy territories …
>
> From captured orders, it emerges that they are instructed not only to tie up prisoners, but also to kill out-of-hand unarmed captives who they think might prove an encumbrance to them, or hinder them in successfully carrying out their aims.

> Orders have indeed been found in which the killing of prison-
> ers has positively been demanded of them.

After declaring the British commandos to be no better than terrorists, the order confirmed what the army had already stipu-lated in its orders from 7 October, just three days after the raid: 'In future, Germany will adopt the same methods against these Sabotage units of the British and their Allies; i.e. that, whenever they appear, they shall be ruthlessly destroyed by the German troops.' On the one hand, Hitler was feigning rage at the breach of the Geneva Conventions by British soldiers. But on the other hand, he was issuing orders to 'ruthlessly destroy' them, which was even more clearly a violation of the laws of war.

This was no longer tit for tat. Hitler was not calling for the commandos to be shackled if captured. He was demanding their *execution*. His order went on to say the following: 'I order, therefore:– From now on all men operating against German troops in so-called Commando raids in Europe or in Africa, are to be annihilated to the last man.'

'*Bis auf den letzten Mann*' – it could not be clearer. But surely Hitler meant in combat, not once commandos had been cap-tured? Not a chance. The next sentences make clear the full horror of the order:

> This is to be carried out whether they be soldiers in uniform, or
> saboteurs, with or without arms; and whether fighting or seek-
> ing to escape; and it is equally immaterial whether they come
> into action from Ships and Aircraft, or whether they land by
> parachute. Even if these individuals on discovery make obvious
> their intention of giving themselves up as prisoners, no pardon
> is on any account to be given.

The execution of British and other Allied soldiers in uniform, following their surrender, would obviously be a war crime. But it was a war crime with which the German military was long familiar. Particularly on the Eastern Front, surrendering to the Wehrmacht had never been a guarantee of safety. It has been estimated that about 60 per cent of Soviet soldiers who surrendered to the Germans died in captivity – a loss of up to 3.5 million lives. The rules of war on the Eastern Front were now to be applied to the West, at least in the case of British and other Allied special forces.

The remaining paragraphs of the Commando Order called on captured commandos to be turned over to the feared SD, Hitler's security service, and under no circumstance to be treated as prisoners of war. Hitler added a final sentence to make clear that he was holding his generals responsible for carrying out the Commando Order, whether they liked it or not, and he had reason to doubt them. In a threatening tone, he wrote, 'I will hold all Commanders and Officers responsible under Military Law for any omission to carry out this order, whether by failure in their duty to instruct their units accordingly, or if they themselves act contrary to it.'

There were apparently additional instructions that the murders would be kept secret, the bodies buried in unmarked graves, and the fate of the captured commandos would not be revealed to the Red Cross or anyone else.

The Commando Order was clearly illegal, and German commanders who enforced it would face war crimes trials after the war, but the reasons for its illegality may not be evident at first. Colonel Scotland, the commander of the London Cage, where prisoners like Obergefreiter Hermann Weinreich were interrogated, had an interesting take on the order:

> Now this decree as it stood was *almost* a legitimate order. According to the accepted rules of conduct in war, there was nothing illegal about the idea of 'no quarter to be given' – in short, a policy of complete extermination of the enemy during combat, a policy that could be applied equally to Commando raiders and to units on any field of battle.

The legitimacy of such an order, however, is determined by one condition: it may be issued by a commander on the strict understanding that its terms are made known not only to his own troops but also to the enemy. What turned the *Befehl* into a totally illegal document was the plain, undeniable fact that it was marked 'Top Secret'. In addition, it was accompanied by a lengthy note of explanation – also top secret – giving the Führer's reasons for the decree. It ended abruptly with the odd statement: 'Should it prove advisable to spare one or two men in the first instance for interrogation reasons, they are to be shot immediately after their interrogation'.

This conclusion seemed strangely contradictory to the terms of the actual *Befehl*. 'It is interesting to recall that both Rommel and Kesselring received the *Befehl* and refrained from passing it on to the officers under their command.'[2]

Though some German commanders like Rommel and Kesselring might reject the illegal order out of hand, most others had no problem with it. Ten days after Hitler issued the order, the killings began. Two weeks before Operation Basalt, a dozen British commandos and two Norwegians went to Norway on a secret mission, code-named Operation Musketoon. It was a raid on the hydroelectric power station in Glomfjord and the mission was a success. After destroying two of the three turbines, they tried to get away by walking to neutral Sweden, but after a mile the Germans caught up with them. Two of the British soldiers were killed. Four made it to Sweden, but six of the team were captured and taken away in chains to Oslo. They were then taken to Germany where they wound up in the Sachsenhausen concentration camp. There, on 23 October, they were shot in the back of the neck and their bodies were cremated. The official line given out by the Nazis was that they had escaped and were no longer held by the Wehrmacht. But in fact, they were the first victims of Hitler's Commando Order.

The German *Kommandant* in Norway, Nicholas von Falkenhorst, 'decided to invest it with a truly lethal force', wrote Scotland, who had interrogated Falkenhorst personally:

> He took it upon himself, indeed, to go one better than Hitler. For in Norway Falkenhorst issued his own version of the *Befehl*, and added to its ruthless character in a peculiarly savage fashion. Riveting his attention on the final words of Hitler's explanatory note, Falkenhorst's order contained the starting new provision: 'If a man is saved for interrogation he must not survive his comrades for more than twenty-four hours.' Not even Adolf Hitler had gone that far in his instructions to the German commanders.
>
> Despite his protestations (how often I had heard such pleas from suspected war criminals) that Hitler's decree had shocked him to the marrow (but of course he 'had no choice' – how often I heard that too!) the case against Falkenhorst when he was tried at Brunswick in July 1946 was heavily weighted by a set of vital documents that were placed before the court – the most damning of these being the voluntary statements he made to me at London Cage during the fortnight following his arrival in England.

While there were some Wehrmacht commanders like Rommel and Kesselring who understood the Commando Order to be illegal, others, such as Falkenhorst, clearly thought it did not go far enough. After the cold-blooded murder of the captured commandos of Operation Musketoon, the Commando Order continued to be carried out with murderous effect. A November 1942 British raid on a heavy water plant in Norway was code-named Operation Freshman. It involved thirty-one men who came in on gliders, which crash-landed. 'Nine survivors from the second glider were put to death after being handed over, on Falkenhorst's instructions, to the Gestapo. Fourteen men from the first glider were shot by troops of the Wehrmacht under Falkenhorst's command.'[3]

If you were a British commando and you fell into German hands, it didn't matter if it was the Gestapo or the Wehrmacht. Both carried out the order with ruthless efficiency.

There were still more killings in December 1942 when Royal Marine commandos were executed by a German naval firing squad in Bordeaux. In July 1943 Norway was again the scene of the execution of Norwegian commandos. American soldiers were among those killed, including Americans serving with the Office of Strategic Services (OSS). Among those who died because of the Commando Order were two of the officers who served on Operation Basalt – Lieutenant Dudgeon and Captain Pinckney, both killed by the Germans following their capture in Italy in 1943.

Many years later, Horace Stokes, who had been one of the raiders that night on Sark, put down his thoughts on the Commando Order. 'Later in the war,' he wrote, 'a number of my very best friends would pay the ultimate price for our raid on Sark, being shot without question, but we were not to know this at the time.'[4] Stokes had been very close to Pinckney and added:

> This made me very angry for a number of years after the war because whilst we may have been tough, ruthless and bloody violent when we needed to be, none of us could have ever executed an unarmed man in cold blood, which is what Hitler had implied for propaganda purposes. At least one man had been shot with his hands restrained but I was unaware of this until we made it back to the boat. The implication that he had been executed was utter bollocks. We were too well trained and disciplined to behave like uncontrolled savages and undisciplined thugs.[5]

The Commando Order was barbaric and it constituted a war crime, but the German response to Operation Basalt did not stop there and the civilian populations of Sark and the other Channel Islands were soon to pay a price as well.

20

COLLECTIVE PUNISHMENT

The German reaction to the raid on Sark has something of the character of Sherlock Holmes' famous 'dog that did not bark in the night'. Initially the Germans were suspicious of the islanders. George Hamon was arrested a few hours after the commando raid while examining his rabbit traps near the Dixcart Valley. He was taken to the *Kommandant's* office. And the two ladies running the Dixcart Hotel, Misses Duckett and Page, were interrogated as well. Many other islanders were questioned. But there were no reprisals.

In her book on the 'model occupation', Madeleine Bunting wrote: 'It has been calculated that if a German was killed in Norway, ten Norwegians were killed in retaliation; in Yugoslavia, a hundred would be killed; in Poland, a thousand.' But when a German soldier was killed in Sark, or three on the night of Operation Basalt, the worst that would happen was 'islanders were deported to German internment camps where they were well fed on Red Cross parcels and survived the war in good health, and no one was killed in retaliation.'[1]

It is possible that the Germans did so little to punish the islanders because this didn't fit into their vision of a 'model occupation' in which the islanders behaved themselves and in turn were largely left alone. It may also have had to do with the fact that they had very little intelligence, at least at first, about the role any islanders may have played on the night of the raid. For several weeks after the raid, despite their suspicions that local people had aided the commandos, suspicions which proved to be well founded, no one on the island had been punished.

Two people, the vicar and Mr Jack Carré, were taken to Guernsey for questioning but were returned to Sark. But on 31 October, Julia Tremayne wrote in her secret letters that Mrs Pittard 'made me a little ginger cake, she came, had a cup of tea and was quite perky and bright but at 10:30 that night the Gestapo, or Military Police, stormed the Jaspellerie and took her off somewhere'.[2] Tremayne herself suspected that Mrs Pittard knew something about the raid long before her arrest by the Germans. 'They are questioning everybody again about it,' she wrote, 'and we think that Mrs Pittard living on top of the bay must know about it, or have aided the landing. That is all we can think at present until we see her again, if we ever do.'

How the Germans came to suspect Mrs Pittard in the first place is a matter of some dispute among historians. According to some reports, she accompanied the commandos from La Jaspellerie to the Dixcart Hotel, to show them the way – and her footprints gave her away to the investigating Germans the next day. This sounds implausible for a number of reasons. First, as the hotel is only a very short walk away from Mrs Pittard's home, it was unnecessary. Appleyard would have known the route from his time on the island on holiday with his family. And second, had this been the case, she would have been arrested within a day or so. But her arrest actually came several weeks later.

Another explanation of how her involvement in Operation Basalt was discovered was the broken glass found by the Germans at her house. She was able to explain that away the first time the Germans spotted it, citing high winds, but eventually the broken window smashed by the commandos gave her away.

And a third explanation is that she eventually turned herself in. The official historian of the German occupation,

Charles Cruickshank, quoted a German description of Mrs Pittard as 'a helpless and somewhat simple-minded woman' and said that she:

> … appeared at the Island headquarters and volunteered the information that she had been awakened by the commandos and had given them a map. When the Germans examined her – and gave her a rough time – they promised that she would not be deported to Germany for more detailed questioning.[3]

The German promise not to deport Mrs Pittard was later to come back to haunt her, as it eventually provided the occupiers with an excuse to commit a far greater crime. Following her admission that she'd aided the commandos that night, Mrs Pittard was taken off to jail in Guernsey. The Germans stood by their promise not to deport her to Germany – for the moment. But the islanders had no idea what had become of her. Two weeks after her arrest, Julia Tremayne wrote:

> There is still no news about Mrs Pittard, no one knows if she is in Guernsey, France or Germany and worse still no one knows what she has been taken away for. We used to read about the Gestapo in Germany taking people off in the middle of their dinner and putting them into concentration camps, but that was mostly for political reasons, but to enter your house and march you off at a moment's notice, without any explanation, is a ghastly thing to do. No one knows whose turn it will be next.[4]

Initially, she was kept in a Guernsey jail in solitary confinement but was later well treated, by all accounts. It took another two months until Mrs Pittard finally returned to Sark, on 18 January 1943. Julia Tremayne was elated: 'Good news! Mrs Pittard came home yesterday, Monday, quite suddenly. She is not allowed to sleep at the Jaspellerie so I suppose she will be watched, but we have not seen her yet.' Later, she added:

Mrs Pittard has been in and looks remarkably well considering her eleven weeks in prison. She says she had good food if
somewhat rough and was well treated, allowed to warm herself by a fire and choose books to read, and looks on it as a
little rest and holiday – some holiday and experience! She is
not allowed to sleep at her home, but can carry on there in the
day time.[5]

Two days after her return to Sark, Mrs Pittard celebrated with
a dinner at the Dixcart Hotel. Miss Page kept a careful record
of all the meals she cooked during that time, and in her tiny
handwriting noted Mrs Pittard's name in brackets and what
she served that night. It was the only reference to a specific
individual at the meals. Because of this, it is known that the
meal celebrating her return home to Sark consisted of cau-
liflower au gratin, carrots, broad beans, potatoes, and gravy.
Dessert was ginger pudding with raspberry sauce.[6]

Later, Tremayne learned more about the circumstances of
Mrs Pittard's arrest. She wrote:

It is known now since we have met Mrs Pittard that our man
actually got into the Jaspellerie and was with Mrs Pittard for
hours getting information about the Germans and their quarters etc. She was asked to leave the Island with them and
refused, wouldn't I like to have had the chance. She tried to
keep it all quiet, but the Germans are like bloodhounds. After
three weeks they carted her off to prison, that is why they sent
for our Vicar and kept him in prison all night. She was supposed
to have told him one or two things.[7]

Little did Tremayne know that Mrs Pittard's return to Sark
would be short-lived, for the Germans had decided the time
had come to punish the islanders for her part in Operation
Basalt. A second round of deportations was about to begin.

On 30 June 1945, not long after the war ended, the Dame of Sark filed a report with the British concerning German war crimes on the island. The report focussed on the two rounds of deportations – the first having taken place just before Operation Basalt and the second several months later. It is worth quoting at some length, as it is the definitive account of the main German war crime on the island:

1 I, Sibyl Mary Hathaway, Dame of Sark, make oath and say as follows: – On the 21st September 1942 I heard that eleven English residents of Sark had received orders to prepare for evacuation to Germany.

Neither I nor the Emergency Committee of which I am President were in any way consulted with regard to the selection of these persons or concerning their deportation which was to Guernsey in the first place en route to Germany. I set out below a list of the persons who were warned, only nine of them were in fact deported for reasons which appear in the list.

3 Mr Moor a gardener and his wife and son aged 11.
1 Mr Jenkins, a farm hand.
2 Mr Thomason, a clerk and his wife.
3 Mr Beaumont, a farmer, and his wife who was in an advanced state of pregnancy, and their daughter aged 7.
Major H.J. Skelton aged 63 and his wife. Major Skelton committed suicide and his wife attempted to do so after receiving the embarkation order. The wife recovered and was not deported.

2 On or about the 15th December 1942 I received a visit from Captain Hinkel the Commandant of the Island who brought with him a list of all the remaining persons resident on the Island. He went through this list with me asking me questions about their employment, character, and means of support. I had no idea why he had brought this list to me, nor what was the reason for his questions.

3 Early in January 1943 I received a visit from Baron von Aufsess who told me that it would be necessary for a number of persons who resided close to the coast of the Island to be evacuated from it. I asked him whether they were to be taken to Germany and he replied that they were to be taken to Guernsey. I told him we could find

alternative accommodation in the centre of the Island for these people, to which he made no reply.

4 I set out below a list of the forty-eight persons who were actually deported to Germany:–

1	Mr R.W. Hathaway, aged 56, Seigneur of Sark.
2	Rev. R.H. Phillips, Vicar of Sark 65 and his wife.
2	Mr R. Wallroth (a very sick man) aged 66 and his wife.
3	Mrs Harriet Mollet, aged 64 a laundress, and two adopted girls.
2	Mr Sharp and his wife a schoolmistress over 60 years.
3	Mrs Lena Gallienne and two children aged 11 and 14.
10	Mrs Hilda Guille, widow, a charwoman and 9 children.
8	Mr Hamon, labourer, his wife and six children, youngest 2½ years.
1	Miss Watts, Boarding house keeper.
1	Mrs Butcher, widow, caretaker.
1	Miss Carter, a retired schoolmistress aged 63.
1	Miss E. Duckett, Hotel Keeper.
1	Miss E. Page.
1	Mrs Campbell widow, aged 63.
1	Miss E. Cheeswright an artist, aged 63.
1	Mr J. Downs, a farm hand.
1	Mr H. Baker, a farm hand.
1	Miss A. Quigley (a domestic servant).
3	Mr E. Falle, his wife who had recently undergone a cancer operation and his daughter aged 17.
1	Mrs Rose Adams, who was pregnant.
1	Mrs Frances Pittard, previously imprisoned by the Germans for speaking to the Commando officers.
1	Mrs Macdill, a cook aged 65.
1	Miss G. Buchan, a domestic servant aged 60.

As the Dame of Sark reported to the British after the war, the Germans decided to deport more than fifty people in February 1943, a far greater number than had been deported in September. The population of Sark at the time was just 413 people.

The deportation of innocent civilians including a large number of children, was a war crime. But why had the Germans done it? The Dame claimed to be unable to explain the German decision to deport so many civilians from Sark. In a document filed with the War Office, she wrote:

> Neither I nor the Emergency Committee were consulted with regard to this deportation or the persons selected for it, and I have always been unable to understand the reasons for it. The persons deported resided all over the Island and not merely on the coast. Some were English born and some were born in the Channel Islands. With the exception of Mrs Frances Pittard they were not persons who were known to have fallen foul of the German Authorities, who had until then left the Island very much to itself.

She later said, 'Sometime later I was told by Colonel Knackfuss that my husband was deported as he was a former British officer, but I was at no time given any reason for the deportation of any of the other persons.'

Though Mrs Hathaway claimed to be 'unable to understand' the deportations, this was not the case for Tom Remfrey. Remfrey was a 10-year-old boy on Guernsey when he was deported to Germany in September 1942, just days before the raid on Sark. He spent the war years with many other Channel Islanders in an internment camp in the German town of Biberbach. Many years later he became chairman of the Guernsey Deportees Association and wrote extensively about the deportations. The wave of deportations that followed the raid were the direct result, he believed, of Mrs Pittard's decision to help the commandos. He wrote that Operation Basalt:

... caused the Channel Island wide reprisal deportations of 'unreliable elements' and others, of February 1943. The unwitting author of these events was 41 year old widow Mrs. Frances Noel Pittard ... Following the raid, and when the raiders' track was discovered, she was questioned by German Military Police who suspected that the raiders had been given information about nearby German sentries and soldiers. Fearful of reprisals against her fellow islanders, she was assured by a German officer that if she told the truth she would not be deported. With this assurance she admitted that the broken glass at her door had been caused by the British Commandos ... According to Wehrmacht records, some agonising took place as whether Mrs. Pittard should be deported to Germany, because of the fact that she trusted in the word of a German officer that she would not be deported. General discussions then took place about the complete evacuation of Sark for military security reasons and which could then include Mrs. Pittard, but this was vetoed because the Germans really needed the islanders to work and maintain Sark for them. It was said that events on Sark showed that the Germans had not yet succeeded in removing 'unreliable elements' from the islands and instructions should now be given as to who should be removed, including Mrs. Pittard.[9]

This seems to be the true explanation. One-eighth of the total civilian population of Sark, including Mrs Pittard, were deported to Germany because the Germans could not deport her alone. And they could not do this because a German officer had given his word that this would be the case. Such was the bizarre thinking in the German Army, with its strange sense of honour, that rather than simply punish the woman who'd aided the British soldiers, they needed to select another few dozen people almost at random to accompany her to Germany.

The Germans gave no 'grounds for deportation' in the case of Mrs Pittard, though they had done so for other deportees. Tom Remfrey speculated:

Clockwise from left: Robert Hathaway, the Seigneur of Sark. One of nearly fifty islanders deported to Germany in the aftermath of the commando raid, the former American consistently defied his captors. (Island Archives, Guernsey)

Mrs Sibyl Hathaway, the Dame of Sark. The feudal ruler of the island, she encouraged islanders not to evacuate when the Germans arrived. (La Société Sercquaise)

The Dame of Sark and her German 'guests', in the Seigneurie. (La Société Sercquaise)

A map of Sark with everything renamed in German. The Hog's Back, where the commandos landed, is labelled here as *Schweinsrücken*. (La Société Sercquaise)

German soldiers relaxing in the Sark sunshine. They considered the island to be a 'little paradise'. (La Société Sercquaise)

German officers on Sark. The *Inselkommandant*, Oberleutnant Heinz Herdt, is standing in the middle. (Doris Theuerkauf)

Oberleutnant Herdt on his horse. To the islanders, he was known as 'Little Steve'. (Doris Theuerkauf)

A view of Sark's east coast, as seen from the Hog's Back. The steep cliffs seemed to provide a natural defence. (Eric Lee)

The eighteenth-century cannon on the Hog's Back mistakenly thought to be a German machine gun emplacement. (La Société Sercquaise)

Petit Dixcart. This was the commandos' 'primary target' but was found to be empty. (Eric Lee)

La Jaspellerie. The commandos' 'secondary target', this too had no German soldiers – but Mrs Pittard, a 40-year-old widow, lived there and provided invaluable intelligence.

Mrs Frances Pittard. 'Is there a fire?' she asked when the commandos broke into her home. (Kevin Adams)

Miss Page, one of the managers of the Dixcart Hotel. (La Société Sercquaise)

Miss Duckett, the other manager. Both women claimed to have slept through the raid that took place only metres away from where they slept. The Germans suspected them of aiding the British. (La Société Sercquaise)

Hubert Lanyon, the baker of Sark. He was eventually arrested and jailed for distributing an underground newspaper on the island. (La Société Sercquaise)

Anderson Manor in Dorset, where the Small Scale Raiding Force lived and trained. (Eric Lee)

Major Geoffrey Appleyard, commander of the Small Scale Raiding Force and leader of the Basalt raid.

Lieutenant Anders Lassen, the legendary Danish commando and future recipient of the Victoria Cross.

Sergeant Joseph Henry 'Tim' Robinson. One of the soldiers of No. 12 Commando, who joined up with the SSRF for the raid. (Graham Robinson)

'We live in deeds, not years'. The only memorial on Sark to the raiders. (Eric Lee)

Even though by helping British Commandos in October 1942, she may have precipitated the clear-out of perceived unde-sirables. This lady served a prison sentence in Guernsey and in return for telling the truth received the word of a German officer that she would not be deported. At least she deserved to be patriotically labelled as 'politically undesirable' or a 'former convict', or did this notable omission satisfy the vaunted German Officers Honour Code?[10]

On the day of the deportation in February 1943, the Dame came down to the harbour to part with her husband and so many of her fellow islanders. As she recalled the day, 'By far the most pathetic figure on the quayside was Mrs Pittard, who had not yet recovered from the shock of her imprisonment in Guernsey and was now about to face an unknown fate in Germany.'[11]

Julia Tremayne also felt sorry for Mrs Pittard, writing: 'I am sorry for poor Frances, apparently they only let her come home for a few days to get her affairs in order, then took her off again, goodness knows to where this time.'[12]

'I made an effort to comfort the mothers,' wrote the Dame in her memoir. She recalls telling them, 'Try not to worry too much about the children. You know the soldiers have been very kind to them here. I spent a long time working in Germany after the last war and noticed how fond the Germans were of children.'[13] At the time Mrs Hathaway was assuring moth-ers taking their small children to an unknown destination that there was little to worry about and that the Germans were fond of children, she could not have been aware that the Holocaust was taking place and would result in the deaths of over a million innocent children.

One of those children deported from Sark that day was Nellie Le Feuvre, whose story, *A Sark Teenager's Deportation*, was privately printed more than sixty years later. Like the Dame, she had no idea why they were singled out for depor-tation. She thought that only English people were being deported, but her family was not English. And she kept a copy of the order she received from the Germans, which ended with this threat: 'Should you fail to obey this order, you must expect to be punished by a martial court.'[14]

Nellie's family were not the only pure-bred Sarkese who were deported to Germany, despite earlier assurances that only English families might be taken. Other families included the Guille and Hamon families, long-established Sark residents. Tom Remfrey asked:

> Was this a mistake or a ruthless and deliberate German tactic designed to intimidate people in Guernsey and Sark once the news had circulated? Or was this a 'last minute' decision by the Germans to wake-up the overall numbers for deportees to around 250 as discussed in the German High Command communications of 30/1/1943?[15]

The German decision to punish Sark for Mrs Pittard's assistance to the commandos spread far beyond the tiny island. In a folio of documents he compiled on the deportations, Remfrey documented the deportations of no fewer than 266 Channel Islanders at this time, taken from all the islands, but mainly from Guernsey and Sark. Remfrey noted that, 'Included in this second wave were 13 British Channel Island Jews (11 from Jersey and 2 from Guernsey). Following their arrival in St Malo, France, and whilst on trains the two groups were unexpectedly and traumatically separated.'[16] Most of the Jews later died in Auschwitz.

The islanders were initially interned at Stalag 122 in Royallieu (France) for about three months, and then moved to ILAG VB in Biberbach (Germany). ILAG is short for *interniertenlager* – an internment camp for civilians. Biberbach had been described as 'a barrack-style prisoner of war (POW) camp'.[17] But according to one account, Biberbach was a place 'where living conditions were quite good and the deportees were allowed to work on the Bavarian farms, whose owners they found generous, charming and friendly'.[18] Nevertheless, more than forty Channel Islanders died in the internment camps at Dorsten, Biberbach, Wurzach and Laufen.[19]

The Dame's husband played an honourable role in the camp. According to one report:

> There were also individuals in the camps who were well known for defying German orders. Among such people we might include Robert Hathaway, Seigneur of Sark, who was sent to Laufen. We are told that for more than two years, he 'refused persistently to obey German orders', 'did his damnedest to make himself unpopular with Germans' and 'occupied himself most of the time by deliberately breaking camp rules'.[20]

The islanders were deported over the course of two days in February 1943. The first group, including Mrs Pittard, left on the 12th. On the following day, Obergefreiter Hermann Weinreich, the German engineer captured by the commandos in the October raid, was also deported, in a sense. He was shipped off from a prisoner-of-war camp in Britain to Canada, where he spent the remainder of the war.

The Germans chose not to publicise this round of deportations, as they had done for the earlier round. It was believed that the Germans feared that if they publicised any of this in their newspapers, the British would find out the same way they did about the earlier deportations, because captured copies of Guernsey newspapers were the source of that information, so few details were given out at the time.[21]

There can be little doubt that the deportations were illegal, and constituted a war crime. As Tom Remfrey wrote:

> It should be noted that the eight criteria for deportation stipulated in the German High Command communications of 27/12/1942 did not demand the deportation and stigmatisation

of dependents and families of those who had given offence, or imagined offence, to the German occupiers of the Channel Islands. This action was typical of the Nazi German 'Sippenhaft' ideology whereby in Nazi Germany the families and relatives of those who opposed, or were thought to have opposed, the Nazi Regime were also persecuted.

It is accepted by both the German and British governments that the deportations from the Channel Islands of civilians was illegal under International Law. Those of February 1943 should have been considered as Nazi and German War Crimes against British subjects who were resident in the Channel Islands and posed no threat to German Occupation Forces.[22]

Deporting innocent civilians, including children, did nothing to increase German security in the occupied Channel Islands. The British Government had no need of local people in order to carry out commando raids, and were already planning the next round.

THE FINAL RAID

Despite the shackling of prisoners and the Commando Order, the operational success of Operation Basalt seemed to have whet the British Army's appetite to try something similar again. There had been proposals to land as many as 120 men on Sark, a force that might have been large enough to overwhelm the German garrison and at least temporarily take control of the island. The recapture of some or all of the Channel Islands had been on Churchill's agenda since the day they fell to the Germans in June 1940.

For example, by 17 January 1943, just three months after Basalt, Operation Bunbury was proposed to retake Sark. In the case of Bunbury, which never took place, the aim was not merely to capture German prisoners. As the proposal read:

> If as a result of our action against Sark, we are able to persuade the Germans to increase their Garrisons in the Cherbourg–Channel Islands area, we shall have succeeded in furthering what must surely be the strategic aim (if any) of our raiding Operations in the Channel (i.e.) to contain German forces and prevent their use on other fronts.[1]

It took the commandos more than a year to return to Sark. The third commando raid on Sark was code-named Operation Hardtack 7 and was timed to coincide with a raid on Jersey.

It began on Christmas night, 25 December 1943, and had an inauspicious start.[2]

Like the previous raid in October 1942, Operation Hardtack 7 failed on the first attempt. Its commander, Lieutenant A.J. McGonigal, reported that their Motor Gun Boat (MGB) arrived just off Sark's Derrible Point at 2345hrs, which was somewhat later than the Basalt raiders. McGonigal was trying a different route. His men, a mixture of British and French commandos, landed in a small craft known as a dory and climbed to the top of a ridge in just fifteen minutes. The ridge 'consisted of a number of pimples connected by narrow ridges', he explained. The commandos climbed up and down and it took them a full hour until they reached the last ridge connecting them to the mainland of Sark. But this ridge, which was just 9m long, was described by McGonigal as 'a knife edge' and 'too sharp to provide a hand grip'. On each side was a sheer drop. McGonigal decided that it could not be crossed.

The commandos then attempted to bypass the ridge. They descended towards the beach somewhat and managed to cross over in a series of stages using toggle ropes. But when they made it across the ridge, they found 'a sheer climb of about thirty feet to the mainland plateau was encountered and was found impossible to climb. Below this there was a sheer drop to the sea.'

By now it was 0200hrs and they'd been on Sark for more than two hours, still not having reached the main part of the island. McGonigal took the decision to withdraw, noting that 'during the whole of this time, although the patrol made a certain amount of noise through loose stones falling over the edge, no signs of enemy sentries or patrols were seen'. An hour later, they were back on board their dory and paddled over to Derrible Bay. McGonigal and Sergeant Boccador decided to check out the beach area. McGonigal wrote that he:

… worked along the cliff edge to the beach moving slowly and carefully since Sergeant Boccador had reported to me that he had seen a sentry patrolling the cliff head over the bay. We eventually reached the end of the rocks. The beach was of shingle and was covered with flat slate-like stone. The sea came up to the cliff edge at this point and from what I could see of the bay, appeared to do so all the way round. There were no signs of mines or wire. I found a small box on the shingle beach which I brought back with me. In order to get at this I had to move for a distance of from five to six feet on the beach and encountered no mines.

McGonigal's conclusion that no mines could be found would later have tragic consequences. But that night, he realised that scaling the cliffs of Sark again would not be feasible. Time was running out. At 0410hrs, Boccador and McGonigal returned to the dory and paddled out to the MGB, which took them back to England.

Like Operation Basalt, Hardtack 7 failed in its first attempt, and like Major Appleyard before him, Lieutenant McGonigal was keen for another go. He got his chance just two nights later. The same force returned to Sark with the same goal: to repeat Basalt's success and capture another German prisoner.

Having decided that the routes he had reconnoitred on Christmas night were not going to get them on to the main part of the island, McGonigal took the decision to follow in the footsteps of Appleyard and go over the Hog's Back. He and his men reported climbing a 60m sheer rock face and then another 30m slope with a shingle, slate and stone surface. They encountered a wire fence, which they cut, and then walked along the path on the Hog's Back as the Basalt raiders had done nearly fifteen months earlier.

McGonigal reported later that he and his men were 'continually searching for mines' as they walked, though the Basalt raiders had encountered none. Eventually they came upon a path that was about 1.8m wide. On both sides of the path was a thick covering of gorse and then a very steep drop. Fearful of discovering mines on the path, they attempted to walk through the gorse, but McGonigal wrote, 'We found that it was impossible to walk through this gorse without making considerable noise and we therefore continued along the path.' This proved to be a fatal mistake.

McGonigal was in the lead, about 15m ahead of his men, feeling for mines, when suddenly two mines exploded behind the patrol. Two of his men, Corporal Bellamy and Private Dignac, were wounded. The first mine exploded less than 1m away from Bellamy, the last member of the patrol, who died within two minutes. The second mine was about 1.5m to the left of it, severely wounding Dignac.

They decided to move the two injured men out of the minefield. McGonigal was again in the lead, still feeling for mines as he walked, but after just a few steps, two more mines exploded, one to his side, and one in front of him. He was injured by the explosions. At this point, the only uninjured member of the patrol was Sergeant Boccador. Dignac was wounded yet again by these additional explosions and died.

McGonigal took the painful decision to leave the two bodies of Bellamy and Dignac where they lay and get back to the boat. But as he later reported, 'No sooner had we started to move, however, than more mines went up all around us. I cannot say how many there were but at the time we had the impression of being under fire from a heavy-calibre machine gun.' It turned out there was no machine gun; the commandos were under attack from German landmines that had been laid on the Hog's Back following Operation Basalt.

In their rush to get back to safety, McGonigal and Boccador left behind a wireless set which had been hidden under a rock and which they were unable to find again, as well as their climbing rope. The explosions of the mines could be heard by many people on Sark that night. But the Germans took their time to respond. It was not until daylight that the Germans found the two bodies of Bellamy and Dignac. The bodies with their blackened faces were taken to one of the buildings near Le Manoir, the German Army's headquarters on Sark. A German officer asked a young Sark girl to look at the faces of the dead commandos to see if they were in any way connected to Sark. They weren't. The two men were then buried in the small military section of St Peter's Church.

Operation Hardtack 7 had been an unmitigated disaster. Two commandos dead, no Germans captured and questions being asked about why the commandos eventually found themselves walking down a heavily mined path that had been used a year earlier by Appleyard and his men. Surely it had been obvious that the Germans were going to place mines there. But McGonigal's after-battle assessment reads almost matter-of-fact:

(a) The first two mines that exploded were behind the patrol and, although we moved about continuously in advance of the two craters, no further mines were exploded. It would therefore appear that we had reached the edge of the minefield and had been unfortunate enough to explode perhaps the last two mines in the field. It is interesting to note that although Sergeant Boccador and myself were feeling our way very carefully, we felt no contact points nor saw any other signs of mines.

(b) All the injuries caused by the exploding mines were sustained by those members of the force who were either standing or kneeling. A person lying flat seemed to be immune from them.

(c) Despite these explosions, no signs of Germans were seen or heard.

(d) There is a mobile searchlight on the island. We saw it as were coming in on the MGB. From 2100 hours until 2140 hours it was turned on every ten minutes and appeared to come from the area of Le Creux Harbour. It was flashed from the cliff top on to the water – the length of beam was approximately 500 yards.

(e) The S-phones we found to be a complete failure.

(f) The felt soled boots were extremely good.

As with Operation Basalt, the British did not publicise the raid and the first reports came from the Germans. Even the first reports in British newspapers relied on German sources. For example, the Manchester *Evening Chronicle* ran the headline 'Commandos Raid Sark, Nazis Say – "Second in three days"'. The article began:

Berlin radio stated to-day that 'a second attempt within the last three days by British Commando forces to land on the Channel Island of Sark has failed. As the enemy neared the beach several detonations were heard and a large flash was observed,' said the radio. 'It can be assumed from this that the mines had done their work. A later check-up confirmed this, and a dead British soldier was found. The German forces did not need to go into action. … A Commando troop, consisting of British and Frenchmen, which attempted to approach our barbed wire entanglements was annihilated,' it was stated.[3]

The Germans gloated. Operation Hardtack 7 had been a debacle. The official German statement read as follows:

The second attempt by the British within three days to land commandos on the Channel Island of Sark failed as did similar attempts. When the enemy approached the beaches several heavy explosions were heard and fires were seen, which allows the conclusion that the mines did their stuff. A later investigation confirmed this. One dead British soldier was found. German defences did not have to go into action.[4]

Germany's allies were similarly pleased with the results. In another report from the German Telegraph Service, datelined Madrid, it read:

O'Crowey, the military correspondent of 'Informaciones', commenting on the situation, notes that in 42 months, the Anglo-Americans have twelve times attacked the Fortress of Europe. The most recent British landing attempt on the island of Sark – a miserable failure – once more confirmed the statements made by leading German personages that the Fortress of Europe is a sure bulwark.

This report was published on 2 January 1944, just five months before the landings at Normandy. As Winston G. Ramsey concluded:

Thus, with an end result worse than on any of the other six raids carried out on the Channel Islands during the Second World War, the last Commando expedition ended in disaster. Altogether, in three year's operations, three Commandos had been killed, one wounded and another eight captured. On balance, therefore, the Commandos possibly won by a hair's breadth but against that one must set the considerable reprisals carried out against the populations – many of whom abhorred the raids.[5]

After the war Dignac's body was exhumed, but Bellamy's remains are still to be found in Sark's cemetery. His gravestone reads: 'BELLAMY R – Mort pour La France, 28.12.43.' After the debacle of Hardtack 7 there were no further commando raids on Sark or any of the other Channel Islands.

REACTION, RESISTANCE, LIBERATION

In a sense, Operation Basalt and Operation Hardtack 7 were not about Sark at all. The commandos didn't come to liberate the island, and only met an islander by chance. In all three commando raids on Sark (including the 1940 landing on Little Sark) on only one occasion did they encounter locals. They came to Sark, as they'd come to the Casquets Lighthouse a few weeks earlier, to capture and kill Germans, although the islanders paid a steep price, especially for the first successful raid in October 1942.

Nevertheless, the commando raids shed light on the life of the islanders under German occupation and this chapter will highlight three aspects of that period on Sark: how the islanders reacted to the commando raids, the organised resistance (such as it was) to German rule, and the liberation in 1945.

Today, Sarkees say that Operation Basalt was welcomed by locals because it showed the island was not forgotten. But at the time, many feared retaliation. As mentioned earlier, in her secret letters, Julia Tremayne wrote, 'I cannot see myself what good the landing down here does ... [the raid] brought us nothing but misery'.[1] The Dame of Sark shared her view, writing in her memoirs that 'it seemed a heavy price to pay for the capture of one prisoner and a copy of the Guernsey Evening Press'.[2]

In one of the earliest accounts of the raid, the Woods' book from 1955, they report on 'a Sark lady [who] still had an aggrieved tone in her voice as she remarked to the present authors: "We were all getting on all right during the Occupation, until the Commandos spoilt everything by coming and murdering two German soldiers."' One is struck today by the use of the word 'murdering' to describe the killing of the Wehrmacht men.

In 1963, with memories of the war still fresh, Michael Marshall wrote that on Sark:

> Many grumbles were heard against the British. One woman is reported to have said: 'We were getting on quite well with the Germans until that beastly raid spoilt everything!' Others felt proud that Churchill had not forgotten Sark, and some hoped the Commandos would come again.[3]

Roy McLoughlin's book, *Living with the Enemy*, has been described as 'the best selling German Occupation title in the Channel Islands ever since with over 70,000 copies sold', and has been reprinted fifteen times. McLoughlin's line is identical to that of earlier authors from the islands. He writes, 'The easy tolerance between Sarkees and Germans favoured a relaxed atmosphere which made daily life less irksome, despite the war and the Occupation. But the Commando raids did much to upset this cosy situation without, as in Guernsey, achieving results of immediate military use.'[4]

He adds that:

> Churchill's eagerness to attack the enemy wherever possible took no account of the consequences of sending spies and commandos into the Islands. Guernsey suffered most. Sark had two commando raids later on in the occupation and one group went ashore on the north coast of Jersey at about the same time without accomplishing anything.[5]

McLoughlin's view that the raids achieved nothing 'of immediate military use' and took place 'without accomplishing
anything' can be challenged today based on what we know
about Operation Basalt. But the views are shared by people
on the islands. John Nettles, for example, is critical of the British
decision to raid Sark. He writes:

> It has been remarked many times and by many authorities that
> the commando raids on the Channel Islands were, to put it
> mildly, not very successful. Little or no useful intelligence was
> gathered, many of the British soldiers were blown up or cap-
> tured, and the civilian population was put at considerable risk.
> As military operations and pin-prick raids, these capture and
> butcher attacks, must be seen as failures.[6]

While this may well have been true of some of the raids on
Guernsey and Jersey, Nettles is keen to specifically criticise the
raid on Sark as well, despite the successful capture of a high-value
prisoner, Obergefreiter Hermann Weinreich, who provided
reams of useful intelligence – as well as the revelations regarding
German war crimes provided by Mrs Pittard. He wrote:

> The Basalt raid had all sorts of nasty consequences for the
> islanders in Guernsey and Sark. Nothing of much importance
> had been discovered, but as a direct result of the action, the
> safety, life and liberty of the Islanders were put even more at
> risk than before. The savage dog was growling.[7]

It may be argued that Julia Tremayne, writing her secret letters during the war, could have no idea what the result of the
raid was. But the Dame of Sark, though she may have been
unaware of the results of the interrogation of Obergefreiter
Weinreich, was surely aware that raid was considered a success and alerted the world to the barbaric German practice of
deporting civilians from the Channel Islands.

And the same may be said of latter-day historians such as Nettles and McLoughlin who, in their eagerness to defend the islanders, find themselves disagreeing with the assessment not only of Churchill but of the entire British military establishment.

Not everyone in the Channel Islands reacted negatively to the raids at the time. Journalist Frank Falla in Guernsey wrote this about the raid:

> Discounting both British and German claims for the raid on Sark, we were quite happy to consider it a success for we saw its results at first hand. It threw every German in Guernsey and Sark into a state of turmoil, bordering on absolute panic … For some time afterwards, the Nazi jitters were with us … The sight or news of any Commando or British serving man landed on our shores was our very lifeblood.[8]

Falla was one of the men behind an underground newspaper on Guernsey known as GUNS (Guernsey Underground News Service). The news-sheet, which gave summaries of the BBC radio news, was published daily from May 1942 until February 1944, when its team was betrayed to the Germans by an Irishman living on Guernsey. When the news-sheet first appeared, it came with the warning, 'Burn after reading'. Possessing a copy, let alone distributing it to others, could incur severe penalties from the Nazis. Falla had an 'old friend' on Sark, the baker Hubert Lanyon, who had worked as a correspondent for The Star. Lanyon almost certainly would have agreed with his positive assessment of Operation Basalt.

In October 1942, Charlie Machon, a 51-year-old linotype operator at the newspaper and one of key members of the GUNS team, came over to Sark from Guernsey for a holiday. Machon met with Hubert Lanyon. During one conversation, Machon opened up to the baker and asked if he would be willing to help distribute their underground publication on Sark. Lanyon had moved to Sark fifteen years earlier when the island was looking for a baker. It turned out that he was excellent at his job, but his somewhat radical politics made him unpopular. His political life included a stint as deputy of the Chief Pleas, the island's parliament, where he was described as a 'progressive' and even a 'radical'.

Lanyon had already been in trouble with the German occupiers. He was hauled before the local authorities for a curfew infraction in June 1941, but insisted in his defence that the church clock was running slow and needed repair. The court agreed, but still fined him and his wife a pound apiece. Lanyon agreed to help Machon and Falla. He would receive a single copy of the GUNS news-sheet and keep it between two children's books, which were part of a lending library he kept in his shop. Trusted people could come in, borrow a book, and with it a copy of the news-sheet. Starved of real news, deprived of their radios and reliant on the heavily censored and pro-Nazi Guernsey newspapers, for about 100 islanders Lanyon's copies of the illegal news-sheet were the only sources of real news.

But it was not only the islanders who were starving for real news. For any underground operating in Europe at that time, if a way could be found to undermine morale among the Germans and stir up trouble in their ranks it would be used. It turned out that the German soldiers on Sark were also keen to know what was really happening in the war, particularly after the tide had turned. According to Lanyon, he could trust some of them with a copy of GUNS. In Guernsey and Jersey at the same time, efforts were being made to stir up mutiny among the occupying troops, though with little success before the end of the war.

In addition to distributing the news bulletin, Lanyon kept an illegal radio in his bakery. He hid it in the prover below his oven, and later claimed that the warmth from the oven kept the batteries working longer.[9] Eventually, Lanyon was caught and taken over to Guernsey for interrogation. He spent forty days in solitary confinement. He was badly beaten, losing some teeth in the process, but never revealed the names of his associates in distributing *GUNS*. Among those he shielded was Cyril Wakely, who brought him the news-sheets hidden on the boat from Guernsey (Lanyon insisted they came by regular post). He denied distributing the news-sheet, claiming that he couldn't trust people on Sark. This was partly true, as he limited the circulation of the bulletin to his closest friends but did not make it common knowledge. On 14 May 1944, he was sentenced to six months' hard labour, but the sentence was eventually reduced to three because his services as a baker were badly needed on Sark.

Lanyon was always modest about his role in the resistance, but after his death, the letters 'G.U.N.S.' were carved into his gravestone, a reminder of his part in fighting back against the Nazi occupiers.

The future that Hitler had imagined for the Channel Islands in 1940 was not to be. The islands were never returned to France, and never turned into resort centres for the 'Strength through Joy' organisation. Instead, they were peacefully handed back to British forces by a broken and hungry German Army. The story of Sark's liberation in 1945 is the story of its occupation in 1940, but told in reverse.

By May 1945, with Hitler dead and German surrender a certainty, both the German soldiers and local civilians awaited the arrival of British forces to Sark. It was not until 10 May that three British officers landed on the island, just as three Germans had done five years earlier. They accepted the surrender of the German forces in Rosebud Cottage next to the German headquarters at Le Manoir. It was possibly the last surrender of German forces in the war, as the Wehrmacht had already capitulated to the Allies on the Continent several days earlier, and in Guernsey the day before.

The British had no troops to spare, so they asked the Dame if she would agree to take charge of the Germans for a few days. She did so, and promptly put them to work. As there were more

In the final weeks of the war, some twenty German soldiers were moved from Guernsey to Sark, where they were billeted in the Arsenal. Both historians writing about these men and one of the museums in Guernsey exhibiting their uniforms have always referred to these as 'Russian' troops. But the name of their battalion was 'Georgier' and their insignia was the red, black and white flag of the independent Georgian republic, which had lasted from 1918 until February 1921 when the country was invaded by the Red Army under Stalin's orders.

They were not Russians, but Georgians, citizens of the Georgian Soviet Socialist Republic. They were captured by the Wehrmacht in Russia while fighting as part of the Red Army and they were given the chance to switch sides, which many of them did. Many Georgians saw their country as occupied territory and there were several bloody uprisings in Georgia against Russian rule.

At the same time as the Georgians were being transferred to Sark, a very large contingent of Georgian troops rose up in rebellion against the Germans on Texel, an island off the Dutch coast. It seems that the Georgians on Guernsey were also getting restless. Just a few weeks later, in early May 1945, anti-Communist Russians serving with the Nazis in Vlasov's army switched sides and helped the Czechs rise up against German rule in Prague. German commanders had good reason to be concerned.

While the end of the war meant German troops could happily return home, for Georgians, Vlasov's men and others it meant being met with special units from SMERSH, Stalin's counter-intelligence unit inside the Red Army. As a result of the Yalta agreement, former Soviet citizens who fell into the hands of SMERSH faced deportation to the Gulag or death upon their return to the Soviet Union.

than 13,000 mines scattered all over the island, they were tasked with clearing them. Within a few days, two of them had died, blown up by their own mines. They were given a military funeral and buried on Sark. Mrs Hathaway remained in charge of the Germans for a full week until British soldiers arrived to take over.

In the immediate aftermath of the liberation, a victory bonfire was lit on the cliffs of the island. It is said that Mrs Hathaway also flew an American flag, a reminder of her husband Bob, the Seigneur of Sark, who was still in Germany awaiting his return home.

Eventually German prisoners of war were put to use not only clearing up the mess they'd made, in particular the mines, but also in fixing La Coupée, the causeway that connects Little Sark to the main island. The road they made with its metal railings still stands today with a plaque commemorating its construction.

British journalists began pouring into the Channel Islands to learn what they had missed in the intervening five years. The commando raid in October 1942 with its revelations about the deportations and suffering on the islands had provided a glimpse, but only a glimpse, into life on the Channel Islands under German occupation.

Mrs Hathaway took the opportunity to spin a 'comic opera' tale of how 'Island Folk Duped Nazis' (as the *Evening Standard* headlined the story). As the journalist wrote:

> It seems like most of the 72 odd Germans on the island were the most gullible people in the world, and the islanders were so astute that they were able to get away with almost anything. They took great delight in appearing as simple folk, but outwitting the 'great brains' of the occupying forces. From what I gather, the Dame decided to be 'tough' with the Jerries from the day they arrived, and she got their respect.[10]

But that narrative would soon be challenged.

JUSTICE

In the immediate aftermath of the war, the Dame of Sark was the subject of an investigation by the Military Investigation Branch. Investigators were looking into the role played by political leaders across the Channel Islands under the German occupation. Like the leaders in Guernsey and Jersey, Mrs Hathaway was never prosecuted. Instead, she was honoured by royal visits shortly after the war. But the initial investigator was scathing in his verdict. He wrote:

> The Dame of Sark, Mrs. R.W. Hathaway, has also been guilty of friendly and ingratiating behaviour towards the Germans. Major Albrech Lanz, the first German *Kommandant* of Guernsey, in his report on the Channel Islands, says that when he landed for the first time on Sark he was very formally and politely received by the Dame, who explained that a large proportion of the Sark people were descendants of the Vikings who came from the far North. After settling official business, Major Lanz and his staff were invited to a good lunch. The Dame was a particular friend of Dr. Maas, Prince von Oettingen, and General von Schmettow, who were frequent visitors at weekends. At Easter 1945, Zachau, Schneeberger and others were invited to a lobster lunch. The Dame of Sark has preserved her property and privileges intact throughout the occupation; her gardens have not even been modified by wartime agriculture.

Since the liberation of the Islands it has become evident that there is a considerable amount of public feeling against the States and the Officials for their behaviour during the occupation, and very great offence was given by the thoughtless official presentation of certain of these people to the King and Queen on their recent visit to the Channel Islands. It is difficult to avoid the conclusion that had Great Britain been defeated people such as Mrs. Hathaway and the Bailiff of Guernsey would have qualified for the title of Quisling.[1]

Many people on Sark today would take issue with that verdict. Most historians have been more generous in their view of her behaviour during the five years that her island was under German rule.

John Nettles writes:

The idea that by treating the German commanders in a civilised fashion they would be encouraged to respond in kind to the benefit of the well-being of the Islanders as a whole did not occur to the rather bleak-eyed officers from British Intelligence … who busily conducted the post-war investigation into charges of collaboration and treason.[2]

There was no follow-up to the British Military Investigation Branch report and no one on Sark or the other Channel Islands was ever punished for collaboration with the Germans. If the question of how to deal with the Channel Islands' leadership was a complex one, the war crimes carried out by the Germans would seem to be a simple matter of identifying the criminals and prosecuting them. But this was not to be the case.

Hitler's Commando Order featured prominently in war crimes trials held after 1945. US Army Colonel Telford Taylor read out the Commando Order in full at the Nuremberg War Crimes Tribunal.[3] He was prosecuting German officers for 'the killing, in violation of International Law and the rules of war, of Allied Commandos, Paratroopers, and members of military missions'.

One of those accused was Generaloberst Alfred Jodl, chief of the Operations Staff of the Armed Forces High Command. His signature on the Commando Order was one of the main charges against him. Jodl tried to use Allied actions to justify the order. These included the binding of prisoners by the commandos during the Sark raid. The court rejected his defence. He was found guilty and sentenced to death. Jodl pleaded to be executed like a soldier by firing squad, but this was rejected. He was hanged on 16 October 1946, almost four years to the day after the order was issued.

The Commando Order also played a prominent role in the trial of the German *Kommandant* in Norway, Nicholas von Falkenhorst. Falkenhorst faced nine charges, the most important of which related to his orders to execute prisoners. He admitted to having received the Führer's order, and told the court: 'I cannot remember the exact wording [of his order] … but I put the last sentence in the following words: "If a man is saved for interrogation, he must not survive his comrades for more than twenty-four hours."'

The Allied prosecutor, Colonel Halse, said this in his closing speech to the court:

> The accused is charged quite definitely and deliberately with being concerned in the killing of those fourteen prisoners-of-war, and, as I said in my opening speech, that was a cold-blooded murder; there was no reason for that murder; the *Führer-Befehl* said nothing about it, and it is my submission that the murder was committed because of the accused's order adding that little paragraph about the stay of execution for twenty-four hours, and it was on that order and that order only that these fourteen men met their death by order of Probst. [Colonel Probst was the chief of staff to General von Behrens, Falkenhorst's area commander in that part of occupied Norway.][4]

The deportations, too, were a German war crime. There is little doubt that the deportations were illegal. According to the UK Government's submission to the United Nations War Crime Commission on 22 May 1945, barely two weeks after the war's end, the deportations were 'breaches of Articles 43, 46 and 50 of the Hague Convention IV, 1907 and General Principles of International law'. They also constituted 'assault and false imprisonment in English law'. In addition:

> Under Law of Guernsey and presumably of Jersey and Sark also, the crime is Assault but would be triable also as a more grave offence under the general jurisdiction of the Courts in respect of all matters of 'malum in se' [evil in itself] which are not the subject of specific law.

The British experts clarified that the deportations were not spelled out as illegal in the Hague Convention. But, they clarified:

> It is true that the offence is not expressly defined in any of these Articles [referring to articles 43, 46 and 50]. But in 1907 respect for life, liberty and humane usages of warfare reached perhaps their highest level … Imagination did not contemplate the German theory of total warfare, and such acts of inhumanity as wholesale deportations, euphemistically referred to in this case as 'evacuation and transfer' were not legislated against. However it seems clear that this offence not only is contrary to the spirit of Hague Convention IV, and general principles of International Law already established, but that the Articles which have been quoted have an application to it in fact and by analogy sufficient to ensure that justice be done even if the charge were not otherwise well founded by inclusion of the offence in list of the Commission's War Crimes which received in effect international sanction as the end of the last Great War.

Whether the 1907 Hague Convention was the legal basis for this or not, they argued that 'no one would dispute that the deportation of these British subjects falls within Crime No. VII of the Commission's list of War Crimes, namely Deportation of Civilians'.

Having determined that the deportations of innocent civilians in the Channel Islands to Germany was a war crime, all that remained was to arrest the German officer responsible and put him on trial.

Though sentenced to death, Falkenhorst's sentence was eventually commuted to twenty years' imprisonment and he was released on health grounds in 1953.

Other German officers whose war crimes trials included references to the Commando Order were General Anton Dostler, who was executed in December 1945 having been found guilty of executing American soldiers, and Kriegsmarine commander Admiral Erich Raeder, who ordered the execution of British Royal Marine commandos and was sentenced to life imprisonment but also released on health grounds in 1955.

Though German officers who carried out Hitler's Commando Order were sometimes punished for their crime, this was not the case with the officers who carried out the illegal deportations on Sark and the other Channel Islands both before and after the October 1942 raid.

General Erich Müller, who had commanded all German forces throughout the Channel Islands until 1943, had been transferred to the Eastern Front and was captured by the Soviets. But the British could not get their hands on him. In October 1947, the office of the Director of Army Legal Services could not 'confirm that General MÜLLER is located in Russia owing to the difficulties of liaison with the authorities there'. The Cold War had already begun and the Soviets were no longer being helpful. By 1949, the file read, 'Unfortunately no further action has been possible in this case since the accused could not be apprehended.' It would seem, wrote one of the British officers, 'that further action for War Crimes is being gradually abandoned'. He was proven correct.[6]

No German officer was ever punished for the deportations of Channel Islanders, in Sark or anywhere else.

EPILOGUE

As the Allies prepared for Operation Overlord, the invasion of Normandy on 6 June 1944, small-scale raiding operations in the Channel Islands and along the French coast were wound down. Most of the men involved in Operation Basalt were moved to North Africa and the Mediterranean:

Major Geoffrey Appleyard was eventually moved to the Mediterranean theatre of operations, where he continued to lead commandos in combat, though the SSRF, which he and Gus March-Phillips had led, was disbanded. By the summer of 1943, Appleyard was the chief of Operational Planning for 2SAS. Though he was taken off operational duty for medical reasons, he still played a key role in planning raids. Appleyard decided to take part in a flight over Sicily as the Allied invasion of that island began, but his aircraft went missing on the night of 12–13 July 1943. His body was never found.

Anders Lassen had a colourful career after leaving the SSRF, leading commandos in combat across the eastern Mediterranean. He was promoted to major, the same rank held by both Appleyard and March-Phillips, and served with No 1 Special Boat Squadron (SBS). He died near Lake Comacchio in Italy on 9 April 1945, just a few weeks before the end of the war. His exploits were legendary and he was posthumously awarded the Victoria Cross for his heroism in Italy.

Captain Philip Hugh Pinckney was killed on 7 September 1943 while on a parachute mission behind German lines in Italy. It is believed that he, as well as other captured commandos, were executed by the Germans despite being in uniform and because of Hitler's Commando Order.

Captain Patrick Dudgeon was also captured and executed in Italy, hundreds of kilometres behind German lines around the same time, another victim of the Commando Order.[1]

Captain Colin Ogden-Smith was killed in action in August 1944 while leading a small commando team behind German lines in France.

Captain Graham Salter Young, the oldest man on the raid, was the only officer involved in Operation Basalt to survive the war, dying in 1972 in Suffolk.

Of the Other Ranks, most seemed to have survived the war as well:

Bruce Ogden-Smith, Colin's younger brother, became renowned for other covert operations during the war, in particular for swimming to French beaches in the dead of night to gather intelligence. This became known as 'beach reconnaissance' and was of enormous value in planning the Normandy landings. At the end of the war, he returned to his home in Wales where he died in December 1986.

Gunner Redborn survived the war and met with Lassen's mother, Suzanne; his account as reported by her is cited by most historians of the raid. (For my own thoughts on Redborn, including whether he actually existed, see Appendix 3.)

Horace 'Stokey' Stokes had an extraordinary career as a commando in the years after 1942, including a long period evading capture by the Germans in Italy, and survived until the 1980s. His memoirs were found by his son and published in 2013.

Tim Robinson continued to serve with commandos in Italy and elsewhere and survived many years after the war.

Corporal Edgar is the only survivor of Operation Basalt still alive today (2015), and he lives in Australia.

Lieutenant Freddie Bourne, the commander of the Little Pisser, survived for many years after the war and gave interviews as late as 1990. These can now be listened to in the Imperial War Museum in London.

★★★

As the whole point of Operation Basalt was to capture a German prisoner, it is surprising how little attention has been paid to him in the literature. The details of Obergefreiter Hermann Weinreich's interrogation, though readily available in the National Archives in Kew, have never been cited. Weinreich's story continued long after his capture that night on Sark. After an initial interrogation at the London Cage, Weinreich was moved around various prisoner-of-war camps in Britain until being shipped off to Canada on 13 February 1943. This was just one day after the second round of punitive deportations of civilians began on Sark. He remained in Canada until August 1946, was returned to Britain and then repatriated to Germany on 27 February 1947.[2]

His three comrades who were killed that evening were buried in the Fort George Military Cemetery in Guernsey: Unteroffizier August Bleyer, age 28, Gefreiter Heinrich Esslinger, age 30 and the sentry knifed by Lassen, Obergefreiter Peter Oswald, age 35.

The only one of the Germans who escaped the commandos unscathed, albeit fully naked, Gefreiter Klotz, was presented with a watch in recognition of his feat. As mentioned earlier, the German High Command praised the outstanding performance of all their men that evening, including the one who surrendered without a fight.

The *Inselkommandant*, Oberleutnant Heinz Herdt, was finally relieved of his command on Sark on 31 December 1943, just days after the failed Operation Hardtack 7. He returned home on leave for the New Year, got engaged and then married in April 1944. He died on 18 February 1977. His daughter, Doris Theuerkauf, apparently still visits Sark regularly.[3]

The Dame of Sark, Mrs Sibyl Hathaway, survived the war and remained the feudal lord of the island until her death on 14 July 1974. She was succeeded in office by her grandson, Michael Beaumont, who remains the Seigneur of Sark to this day.

The fate of Mrs Frances Pittard, the brave woman who gave so much useful information to the commandos, has been something of a mystery for many years. At the end of the war in 1945, it was not at all clear what had become of her. A May 1945 newspaper story was headlined 'Stories of Two Brave Women of Sark – One Helped Raiding British Commandos', and it told a version of Mrs Pittard's story. 'Two women of Sark will find an imperishable place in the history of these islands. They are white-haired, elderly gracious ladies, with a courage that outlives the years,' it reported. The fact that Mrs Hathaway was old enough to be Mrs Pittard's mother was not noted as the latter continued to be referred to as 'elderly'.

The Dame of Sark told the journalist the story of Mrs Pittard as she understood it. 'She is Mrs. Pittard, widow of Doctor M. Pittard, of Cardiff, and she is over 60, said the Dame … [the Germans] arrested Mrs. Pittard, sent her to prison, and then deported her to Germany. We are praying that she is safe in England.'[4]

A later newspaper account, headlined 'S.O.S. for heroine of Sark', began her story with these words: 'In the Channel Islands, they are waiting to welcome back an elderly, white-haired woman who may never come back, but whose bravery will live on in the story of Sark Island.'[5]

Four years after the war had ended, Anders' mother, Suzanne Lassen, wrote:

> When at long last Sark was liberated, it was learnt that after the attack, the Germans had scoured the island. They found their

way to the house of the English woman. They had questioned her about the splintered glass and various marks around the house; as a result, she had been deported to Germany. Not a word has been heard of her since. She is one of this war's many martyrs, and in the eyes of the people of Sark, a saint.[6]

But it turned out that reports of Mrs Pittard's demise were somewhat exaggerated. The first evidence that she arrived safely in Germany with the other deportees is a postcard she wrote to her friend John Hamon on Sark in May 1943. In it, she wrote:

Dear John, Your letter of April 26th received today. Very glad to hear from you and know you are still looking after the gardens. I was very happy to hear darling Taffy is well and that Jilt has had her baby, it sounds sweet. Every day I think of Sark and you all and long for my quick return. We had a very hot spell of weather, then a cold patch with 2 days rain, now sunny again. I keep very well and hope to hear from you soon. Best wishes, Frances Pittard.[7]

Though her name didn't appear on the Channel Islands Refugees Committee's 'List of Persons Deported from the Channel Islands to Germany', which runs on for thirty pages, it does appear on a handwritten list of people detained in Biberbach in December 1943. The first clue that she survived Biberbach is her absence from a published list of Channel Islanders who died while in Germany.[8] Nor does her name appear on the memorial to islanders who died in Biberbach.[9] The more one digs in the archives, the more evidence appears that Mrs Pittard not only survived the war, but returned to Sark.

In 1950, Frithjof Saelen, a Norwegian author writing a biography of Lassen, wrote to the Dame of Sark asking some questions and passing on information he'd gathered about the 1942 raid. In a handwritten PPS he added, 'Do you think Mrs. Pittard, the doctor's wife, could give a description of her meeting with the commandos? And also what kind of information she gave them?'[10] And *The Fief of Sark*, a record of land holdings on the island published in 1969, recorded that La Sablonnerie, on Little Sark, had been purchased by Ernest George Mardon, Frances' father, in 1920, and that his 'daughter Mrs Pittard, sold it in 1946 to Philip Perree, the present owner'.[11]

Islanders tell the story that she indeed returned to Sark to live there, forming a romantic attachment to a Mr Norris. Later she changed her name to Frances Norris by deed poll, though they never married. Islanders also say that one of the commandos (one story is that it was Major Appleyard, but that is clearly wrong) visited her many years later on Sark. As the story goes, the commando told her that every time they met, she seemed to be in her nightclothes.

As I discovered in February 2015, Mrs Pittard is buried in the Sark cemetery, having died in 1969. Her grave is just above and overlooks the graves of Robert Hathaway and his wife Sibyl, the Seigneur and Dame of Sark.

APPENDIX I

CHRONOLOGY OF THE RAID

Sark under German occupation was required to use German time, but the times below are British, as these mainly come from the reports filed by the commandos.

3 October 1942

1903hrs	MTB 344, known as 'Little Pisser' with a dozen commandos on board departs from Portland. Lieutenant Freddie Bourne is in command of the boat.
1920hrs	The boat passes Portland Bill and enters the English Channel.
2053hrs	They pass Casquets Rock, scene of the earlier, highly successful commando raid known as Operation Dryad.
2117hrs	To avoid detection, they reduce speed on the main engines to 10 knots as they come close to Sark.
2130hrs	They spot a red light flashing and confirm it as coming from Sark.
2220hrs	They are now 6km east of the southern tip of Sark and cut off main engines, slowing down to 5 knots on the silent auxiliary engines.

2245hrs	They can see the coastline of Sark quite clearly now.
2310hrs	MTB *344* drops anchor off of Pointe Château, on the east coast of Sark.
2312hrs	The Goatley craft is launched from MTB *344*, with the twelve commandos on board. Anders Lassen pilots it towards shore.
2320hrs	They land off Pointe Château but realise that they've landed on a rock offshore rather than the island itself; the men are then re-embarked on the Goatley.
2330hrs	The commandos finally land on Sark. Ascent of the cliff begins, with Lassen rushing up first.
0000hrs	The whole party assembles on top of the cliff. They quickly come across what appears to be a German patrol, but it turns out to be dummies on a firing range.

4 October 1942

0115hrs	The raiders reach Petit Dixcart, a small cluster of houses in a wooded valley. The houses are empty.
0135hrs	They reach a large house, La Jaspellerie, but cannot find a way in.
0150hrs	They finally break into the house and awaken Mrs Frances Pittard, and then spend the better part of an hour with her. On her advice, they leave for the Dixcart Hotel Annexe where five German engineers are billeted.
0245hrs	Shooting is heard after the commandos first kill a sentry and then capture five other soldiers, several of whom attempt to escape.
0310hrs	The commandos and their prisoner reach the top of the cliff and begin their descent, helped by the bright moonlight.
0335hrs	They reach the Goatley and row out to rendezvous with MTB *344*.

0345hrs   MTB *344* begins to head back to Portland with everyone on board.

0605hrs   They make landfall at Portland Bill.

0633hrs   They reach Portland Harbour safely, and turn over their prisoner to MI19.

APPENDIX 2

THE COMMANDO ORDER

Der Führer
F.H.Qu., 18.10.1942
Nr. 003830/42 g.Kdos.OKW/WFSt.

12 Copies

Paragraph 1

For some time our enemies have been using in their warfare, methods which are outside the International Geneva
Convention. Especially brutal and treacherous is the behaviour
of the so-called Commandos who, as is established, are partially
recruited from freed criminals in enemy countries. Their captured orders divulge that they are directed not only to shackle
prisoners but also to kill defenceless prisoners on the spot,
the moment they believe that the latter represent a burden
in further pursuance of their purpose or can otherwise be a
hindrance. Finally, orders have been found in which the killing of
prisoners had been demanded on principle.

Paragraph II

For this reason it has already been announced in an addendum to the Armed Forces Report of 7.10.1942 that in future Germany in the face of these sabotage troops of the British and their accomplices will resort to the same procedure, i.e., that they will be ruthlessly mowed down by the German troops wherever they may appear.

Paragraph III

I therefore order that from now on all opponents brought to battle by German troops in so-called commando operations in Europe or Africa, even when it is outwardly a matter of soldiers in uniform or demolition parties with or without weapons, are to be exterminated to the last man in battle or while in flight. In these cases it is immaterial whether they are landed for their operations by ship or aeroplane or descend by parachute. Even should these individuals, on their being discovered, make as if to surrender, all quarter is to be denied on principle. A detailed report is to be sent to the OKW on each separate case, for publication in the Wehrmacht communique.

Paragraph IV

If individual members of such commandos working as agents, saboteurs, etc., fall into the hands of the Wehrmacht by other means, such as through the police in any of the countries occupied by us, they are to be handed over to the SD immediately. It is strictly forbidden to hold them in military custody or in a prisoner of war camp, even as a temporary measure.

Paragraph V

This order does not apply to the treatment of any enemy soldiers who in the course of normal hostilities (large-scale offensive actions, landing operations, and airborne operations) are captured in open battle or give themselves up. Nor does it apply to enemy soldiers falling into our hands after battles at sea or trying to save their lives by parachute after an air battle.

Paragraph VI

In the case of non-compliance with this order, I shall bring to trial before a court-martial any commander or any other officer who has failed to carry out his duty in instructing the troops about this order or who has acted contrary to it.

Signed: Adolf Hitler

Distribution:

OKW – *Oberkommando der Wehrmacht* (High Command of Army, Navy and Air Force)
C-in-C Norway
C-in-C South East
High Command West
High Command South
High Command Twentieth Mountain Army
Panzer Army Africa
Reichführer SS
Chief of SIPO

The German text can be found here: www.documentarchiv. de/ns/1942/kommandobefehl.html. There is an English translation in Le Tissier, *Mined Where You Walk*, pp. 128–129.

APPENDIX 3

WHO WERE THE RAIDERS?

Who were the British commandos who carried out the raid on Sark? As there were only a dozen of them, and the raid is fairly well documented, this would seem to be an easy question to answer. But it is not. I have not been able to locate, in any archive, a definitive list of all twelve men. It is very clear who the officers were on the raid: every source agrees that Appleyard, Pinckney, Dudgeon, Lassen, Young and Ogden-Smith were there. The problem arises with the Other Ranks, referred to as ORs in the records. The official reports give no names.

The closest thing to a primary source listing who participated in the raid is an entry in Colin Ogden-Smith's handwritten diary. Peter Jacobs, who wrote about Ogden-Smith's extraordinary war record, shared the page with me, and here is Ogden-Smith's list of who participated in Operation Basalt:

Major Appleyard
Captain Pinckney
Dudgeon
Lassen
Young
Myself
Bruce
Edgar

He then lists the following four names and indicates that they are all from No. 12 Commando.

Sergeant Thompson
Brigadier Flint
Private Forster
Greenfield

As Jacobs points out, there are a couple of differences between this list and his list of who went on the abortive raid of 19–20 September. One of those who went on the earlier raid but is not listed here is Horace Stokes. Jacobs explains:

> I suspect the names that are unfamiliar to you are some of the 12 Commando names – Thompson, Foster (could be Forster) and Greenfield, but they are definitely shown in the diary. Colin was good at keeping his diary but he was clearly tired by this phase of the war as his entries are shorter than they were with Layforce in 1941 for example. He may have recorded these names in his diary later, although his entry for 4/5 Oct is clearly written with a different pen (colour of ink) from his entry on 19/20 September and so it is not as if he wrote up the two nights at the same time. Some of the 12 Commando Other Ranks would have been new to him and so there could be errors with the names but in the rest of his diary, where he does not remember a name, he has simply used their rank (e.g. see entry for 19/20 Sep).[1]

Brian Lett, who authored the definitive book on the SSRF, is not convinced by Ogden-Smith's list. For one thing, Ogden-Smith may not have known the names of all the men in Pinckney's unit, as Jacobs concedes. 'I do not think he knew the names of the Other Ranks who had recently joined from 12 Commando. Why should he?' he writes.[2]

Leslie W. 'Red' Wright claimed to have participated in the Sark raid, and he is the source of the story about the retrieval of a Polish SOE agent from the island. That story is repeated in numerous accounts of the Sark raid. But Wright's claims have been thoroughly debunked by Lett in an appendix to his book on the SSRF entitled 'The Man Who Was Not There'.[3]

More problematic is the case of Gunner (or Bombardier) Redborn (sometimes spelled Redbourn and Redbourne). His first-hand account of the raid, which appears accurate, is cited by Lett and many other authors and seems to originate in an early post-war account published by Anders Lassen's mother, Suzanne.

Here is what she wrote about him:

> All three officers who took part in this raid are dead, and the following account has been furnished by a private soldier, Gunner Redborn. Redborn is small and modest with a big black moustache, and as he calmly and authoritatively relates his stirring experiences in the Commando forces, one is startled to learn that in civilian life he is a milliner.[4]

Most accounts agree that he came with Pinckney and No. 12 Commando. The only problem is, there doesn't appear to be much additional evidence that he existed and it is possible that Mrs Lassen was using a false name to protect his testimony.

Another problem is the role of Sergeant Horace Leonard 'Stokey' Stokes, who was definitely part of No. 12 Commando. Stokes clearly participated in the first attempt to land commandos on Sark in September 1942, as Ogden-Smith's diary records. Stokes is author of a memoir, *No Ordinary Life*, published posthumously in 2013, which recounts his experience during the raid on Sark – both the abortive one, and the actual raid in October. His account of the raid, like Redborn's, matches others and seems quite accurate (except for his description of Mrs Pittard as the Dame of Sark). But he does not appear on Ogden-Smith's handwritten list for the second raid.

Another commando serving under Pinckney throughout the war was Sergeant Joseph Henry 'Tim' Robinson and he was close friends with Stokes. Robinson's son, Graham, is convinced that both his father and Stokes participated in the Sark raid and agrees with Lett that as Ogden-Smith did not know the new men who came over from No. 12 Commando, he may well have had some of the names wrong. For example, Thompson (a name which, like Redborn, does not appear in any records of E Troop 12 Commando) could be Robinson, he says. In addition to his father's own testimony to his family throughout his life, Robinson has collected a great deal of circumstantial evidence pointing to his father having participated in the raid. Lett is convinced that Robinson is correct and that Tim Robinson participated in the raid, as did Horace Stokes.

Graham Robinson says he asked the last surviving member of the raiding party that night, Corporal Edgar, what he could remember. Unfortunately, Edgar could not tell him who was on the raid after so many years.[5]

Lett concludes that some of:

> ... those who went on the operation may not have wanted to tell the truth about what happened, or being a part of it, particularly after the war when the Nuremburg trials took place. To shoot prisoners whose hands are tried is, *prima facie*, a war crime. Also, of course, all those who worked with SOE and the SSRF had signed the Official Secrets Act – even the men of 12 Commando, I believe.

Among others, Dudgeon told a relative that he was 'embarrassed about having been involved – perhaps because of the Commando Order that resulted'.[6]

After more than seven decades, I have reached the conclusion that we may never know with absolute certainty who were the twelve men of the SSRF and No. 12 Commando who landed on Sark that night in October 1942.

NOTES

PRELIMS

1 WO 311/105.
2 Durand, p.119.
3 Durand, p.119.

CHAPTER 1

1 Bunting, p.289.
2 Le Tissier, *Island Destiny*, p.26.
3 Baron von Aufsess, *The von Aufsess Occupation Diary*, edited and translated by Kathleen J. Nowland (Chichester: Phillimore, 1985) pp. 97–98.
4 Von Aufsess, p.103.
5 McLoughlin, p.201.

CHAPTER 2

1 Hathaway, p.112.
2 Hathaway, p.116.
3 Oddly, the German aircrews reported that this firing came from the actual island of Sark. This was repeated by German Admiral Schuster in his war diary.
4 Hathaway, p.116.
5 Marshall, p.8.
6 Hathaway, p.112.
7 This and the following quotes from Hitler, *Hitler's Table Talk*, p.584.

8   Briggs, p.13.
9   Nettles, p.157.

CHAPTER 3

1   Marshall, p.11.
2   Marshall, p.10.
3   Marshall, p.11.
4   Hathaway, p.117.
5   Hathaway, p.114.
6   Hathaway, p.117.
7   Hathaway, p.118.
8   Hathaway, p.118.
9   Hathaway, p.120.
10 Marshall, p.13. It is not known what the Foreign Office replied, if it replied.
11 Marshall, p.14.
12 Moreman, p.53.
13 Le Tissier, *Mined*, p.62. Ramsey writes that 'the men arrived on another island believed to be Sark' (p.137).
14 Moreman, p.54.
15 Interview with Richard Dewe, 6 February 2015.
16 Interview with Werner and Phyllis Rang, February 2015.
17 Niven, David, p. 480. It seems this was the version he heard of the July 1940 raid. The pub visit may have been a bit of artistic licence.
18 Stephenson, p.12.
19 Interview with Mrs Esther Perree, 10 February 2015.
20 Hathaway, p.132.

CHAPTER 4

1   Hathaway, p.121.
2   Hathaway, p.129.
3   Hathaway, p.130.
4   Hathaway, p.130.
5   McLoughlin, pp.67–68.
6   Marshall, p.16.

7   Marshall, p.15.
8   Cited in Nettles, p.74.
9   Hathaway, p.127.
10 Tremayne, p.117.
11 McLoughlin, p.125.

CHAPTER 5

1   Two decades earlier, she was living in Germany and her husband,
    Dr Wranowsky, delivered a baby. His name was Werner Rang and
    in a remarkable coincidence, he arrived on Sark as a Wehrmacht
    medical orderly in 1942. Le Tissier, *Island Destiny*, p.35.
2   Fraser, pp.30–31.
3   Island Archives, Guernsey, CC/3-20. It is not clear if this was a
    German or Czech passport.
4   Fraser, pp.30–31.
5   Cohen, p.48.
6   Fraser, p.31.

CHAPTER 6

1   Konstam, p.37. Strangely, Konstam in his book on British Motor
    Torpedo Boats gives what appears to be a definitive list of the
    boats – but writes that 'The pennant numbers "332–346" were
    allocated to Vosper, but were not used.' Clearly number '344' was
    used, as photographs show.
2   IWM – Oral History 11721. Interview with Frederick William
    Parnell Bourne – by Conrad Wood, for the IWM – on
    15 November 1990.
3   Appleyard, pp.12–13.
4   Appleyard, p.21.
5   Appleyard, p.47.
6   Appleyard, p.49.
7   Appleyard, p.50.
8   Appleyard, p.54.
9   HS 9/1377/2.
10 Cited in Keene, p.183.
11 Stokes (ebook), loc. 504.

12 WO 373/93/1439
13 Cited in Lett, p.34.
14 For a full discussion of who participated in the raid, see Appendix 3.

CHAPTER 7

1 From a folio of documents relating to the deportations donated by Remfrey to La Société Sercquaise.
2 WO 311/105.
3 Island Archives, CC 04-26.
4 Hathaway, p.141.
5 Hathaway, p.140.
6 This letter can be found in the archives of La Société Sercquaise, but neither they nor the archives of the Seigneurie contain Major Skelton's 1942 messages.
7 Interview with Richard Dewe, a member of the Channel Islands Occupation Society, in Sark, 6 February 2015.
8 Le Tissier, *Mined*, p.57.
9 Interview with Richard Heaume, German Occupation Museum, Guernsey, 11 February 2015.
10 William M. Bell, *Guernsey Occupied but Never Conquered*, privately printed in 2002, pp.226–227.
11 Nettles, p.96. I can find no evidence to back up the story that Skelton was Jewish.
12 Le Tissier, *Mined*, p.58.
13 McLoughlin, p.122.
14 Hathaway, p.135.

CHAPTER 8

1 Tremayne, p.160.
2 Stokes (ebook), loc. 686.
3 Bunting, p.50.
4 Bunting, p.243.
5 WO 218/41. This then refers to S.T.S. 62 War Diary.
6 Wood, Jenny, *Herm, Our Island Home* (London: Robert Hale, 1972) p.14.

7   Keene, p.178.
8   Appleyard, p.129.
9   *La Trobe Guide*, p.43.
10 *La Trobe Guide*, p.43.
11 Unfortunately, I was not able to find evidence of this in the official record of Operation Dryad in DEFE 2/109. According to a report there, he is not listed as having actually served on Sark.
12 Saelen, p.1.
13 Cruickshank, p.203.
14 Stokes (ebook), loc. 692.
15 Stokes (ebook), loc. 697.
16 Stokes (ebook), loc. 702.

CHAPTER 9

1   Le Tissier, Mined, p.64.
2   Saelen, p.1.
3   Marshall, p.26.
4   DEFE 2/109. Appleyard's four-page report after the raid.
5   DEFE 2/109.
6   DEFE 2/109.
7   Saelen, p.2.
8   Stokes (ebook), loc. 719.

CHAPTER 10

1   DEFE 2/109.
2   Stokes (ebook), loc. 719.
3   Ramsey, p.149.
4   Marshall, p.26.
5   Saelen, p.2.
6   Saelen, p.1.
7   Appleyard, p.130.
8   DEFE 2/109.
9   Saelen, p.3.

CHAPTER 11

1   DEFE 2/109.
2   Le Tissier, *Mined*, p.66.
3   Nettles, p.197. The story is also told by Ramsey, p.160. He
    writes, 'She was obviously very nervous and when they asked
    the whereabouts of any Germans, she said she could not help.
    Instead, she directed them to another farm where she said they
    might get the information they required.'
4   Saelen, p.3.
5   Saelen, p.4.
6   DEFE 2/109.
7   Saelen, p.4.
8   DEFE 2/109.
9   DEFE 2/109.
10 Stokes (ebook), loc. 734.
11 Keene, p.182. He cites a statement by James Edgar to the author.
12 Le Tissier, *Mined*, p.66.
13 Email from James Edgar to the author, 19 May 2016.
14 Saelen, p.5.

CHAPTER 12

1   According to one account (Marshall, pp.27–28), Lassen did
    not kill the sentry outright, but 'fearing the man might regain
    consciousness he had had bound his arms and legs with a toggle
    rope'. No other account confirms this.
2   Strangely, in his very detailed report on the raid, Appleyard made
    no mention of Lassen's killing of the German sentry.
3   Lassen, p.55.
4   Saelen, p.6.
5   Presumably he means five.
6   Lassen, p.55.
7   Forty, p.194.
8   Saelen, p.6.
9   Saelen, p.7.
10 Lassen, pp.55–56.
11 DEFE 2/109.

12 Keene, p.186. Keene is quoting Ian Warren, an SSRF officer who
    was not on the raid to Sark but who discussed it the next day
    with Captain Dudgeon.
13 DEFE 2/109.
14 http://users.skynet.be/albertengel/Guernsey/sark_operation_
    basalt.htm.
15 DEFE 2/109.
16 Keene, p.185.
17 Stokes (ebook), loc. 755.
18 Wood, p.142.
19 He showed it to Winston Ramsey, who photographed it.
20 Saelen, p.7.
21 He probably means one of the Ogden-Smiths.
22 Lassen, p.56.
23 Saelen, p.7.
24 Lassen, p.57.
25 Keene, p.187.
26 Lassen, pp.57–58.
27 Wood, p.144.
28 Appleyard, p.128.

CHAPTER 13

1   Forty, p.194.
2   Forty, p.195.
3   Lassen, p.56.
4   Keene, p.185.
5   Marshall, p.29.
6   Stokes (ebook), loc. 755.
7   Ramsey, p.155.
8   Marshall, p.30.
9   Tremayne, pp.101–102.

CHAPTER 14

1   Jacobs (ebook), loc. 1408.
2   Wood, p.145.
3   Appleyard, p.128.

4   Appleyard, p.132.
5   DEFE 2/109. Preliminary Interrogation of P/W Hermann WEINREICH at the London District Prisoner-of-War Cage.
6   See DEFE 2/109, 'Additional Report on P/W Hermann Weinreich', dated 11.10.42.

CHAPTER 15

1   Marshall, p.31.
2   *The Star*, 8 October 1942, p.1.
3   *Guernsey Press*, 9 October 1942, p.1.
4   WP 43 (4), 3 January 1943, War Cabinet. 'Shackling of Prisoners of War. Official statements by His Majesty's Government'.
5   Cited in Lett, p.121.
6   *The Star*, 13 October 1942, p.1.
7   *The Star*, 13 October 1942, p.1.
8   Durand, p.120.

CHAPTER 16

1   Cruickshank, p.203.
2   Marshall, p.30.
3   Tremayne, p.105.
4   DEFE 2/241.
5   Marshall, p.30.
6   *Channel Islands Occupation Review* (CIOR), vol. 27, p.13.
7   Letter to the author, 27 February 2015.
8   Interview with Richard Heaume, February 2015.

CHAPTER 17

1   Bunting, p.231.
2   WO 311/105
3   Bunting, p.231.

CHAPTER 18

1 Cruickshank, p.204.
2 DEFE 2/109.
3 Cruickshank, p.204.
4 Lett, p.122.
5 *Time*, 26 October 1942.
6 Cited in Keene, p.187. His source is a letter from Mountbatten at the Broadlands Archive, Hartland Library, University of Southampton.

CHAPTER 19

1 Also known as the *Kommandobefehl*; sometimes known as the *Führer-Befehl*.
2 Scotland, pp.164–166.
3 Scotland, p.167.
4 Stokes (ebook), loc. 761.
5 Stokes (ebook), loc. 766.

CHAPTER 20

1 Bunting, p.328. Her account of the German death is confused and inaccurate; she conflates the murdered doctor with the commando raid, getting the year wrong on that, and gets the number of deportees wrong. But her point is an important one; there was no serious cost to the islanders for the commando raid.
2 Tremayne, p.104.
3 Cruickshank, p.204.
4 Tremayne, pp.104–105.
5 Tremayne, p.114.
6 Archives of the Seigneurie, Sark, F.4.503.2.
7 Tremayne, p.105.
8 WO 311/105.
9 Remfrey, Folio 1.
10 Remfrey, Folio 2.
11 Hathaway, p.151.

12 Tremayne, pp.117–118.

13 Hathaway, p.152

14 Reproduced in Le Feuvre, p.4.

15 Remfrey, Folio 3.

16 Remfrey, Folio 1.

17 Carr, p.139.

18 Marshall, p.37.

19 Remfrey, Folio 8.

20 Carr, p.140. His source is Marshall's *Hitler Invaded Sark.*

21 Durand, p.121.

22 Remfrey, Folio 7.

CHAPTER 21

1   DEFE 2/141.

2   Most of this is the report by Lieutenant A.J. McGonigal, as cited in Ramsey, pp.165–167.

3   *Evening Chronicle*, 29 December 1943.

4   DEFE 2/241.

5   Ramsey, pp.165–167.

CHAPTER 22

1   Tremayne, p.160.

2   Hathaway, p.145.

3   Marshall, p.32.

4   McLoughlin, p.122.

5   McLoughlin, p.27.

6   Nettles, pp.158–159.

7   Nettles, pp.194–195.

8   Falla, p.80.

9   Most of this story comes from an article by E. Le Feuvre for *Channel Island Life*, written around 1960. The original text was found in the archives of La Société Sercquaise.

10 *Evening Standard*, 23 May 1945.

CHAPTER 23

1 HO45/22399.
2 Nettles, p.62.
3 http://www.nizkor.org/hweb/imt/tgmwc/tgmwc-04/tgmwc-04-28-01.shtml.
4 Scotland, p.169.
5 TS 26/337.
6 WO 311/105.

EPILOGUE

1 His file at the National Archives (HS9/454/3) reports him as being missing from a secret SAS operation, with no further details.
2 Weinreich's P.W.IB. Form No. 2, from the Deutsche Dienststelle für die Benachrichtigung der nächsten Angehörigen von Gefallenen der Ehemaligen Deutschen Wehrmacht (WASt).
3 CIOR, vol. 27, p.13.
4 *The Evening News*, Portsmouth, 24 May 1945.
5 *Egyptian Gazette*, 1 June 1945.
6 Lassen, p.57.
7 Photocopy of postcard, La Société Sercquaise.
8 Harris, pp.210–211.
9 Le Feuvre, p.21. There is a photograph of the memorial here and Pittard does not appear.
10 Frithjof Saelen to Sibyl Hathaway, the Dame of Sark, 12.7.1950. La Société Sercquaise.
11 Ewen and De Carteret, p.131.

APPENDICES

1 Email correspondence with the author.
2 Email correspondence with the author.
3 Lett, p.194.
4 Lassen, p.51.
5 Email correspondence with the author.
6 Email correspondence with the author.

SOURCES AND FURTHER READING

A list of key primary and secondary source materials for those who want to learn more. More information on sources can be found at http://www.operationbasalt.com.

PRIMARY SOURCES

Imperial War Museum (IWM)
Oral History – 11721: Interview with Frederick William Parnell Bourne by Conrad Wood, for the IWM, on 15 November 1990. This was quite useful as Bourne discusses in some detail the various commando raids.

Oral History – 12542: Interview with Philip Perree, a Sark fisherman, eyewitness to the aftermath of the December 1943 commando raid on Sark.

Oral History – 31334: A second interview with Freddie Bourne, done by the Coastal Forces Heritage Trust, covering much of the same ground as the first.

Island Archive, Guernsey
Contains numerous records relating to the German occupation of the Channel Islands, with some material on Sark. These

include registration records, with photographs, of everyone on the island. The letters exchanged between island officials and the Germans regarding the registration of Jews – of which there appears to have been only one on Sark – illustrate an important point about the German occupation which is often overlooked.

National Archives

ADM 179/228 – This is the navy's file on Basalt, and contains reports found elsewhere.

DEFE 2/45 – This folder contains nothing on Basalt, but some material on No. 12 Commando, some of whose members participated in the raid. The same material – the originals – can be found in WO 218/41.

DEFE 2/98 – This thin folder contains, among other things, the first report received on the Sark raid, dictated by Captain Appleyard over scrambler telephone.

DEFE 2/109 – This large bound volume contains a number of very useful records, including Appleyard's full report on the raid, the reports of intelligence officers, etc. It also contains a report on Operation Musketoon, whose participants were among the first victims of Hitler's Commando Order. The reports on Operation Dryad contain a summary of the intelligence gathered on that raid, but give no indication if any of it related to the Sark raid which followed.

DEFE 2/101 – Operation Hardtack 7 – the failed follow-up raid on Sark in December 1943. The first page is a report on Operation Basalt, laying out where the landmines would be – mines which killed two of the commandos in this raid. In fact, much of what is in this folder relates to Basalt, from lessons learned (or not learned) from that raid.

HS 9/454/3 – Records for Patrick Dudgeon.

HS 9/1376/7 – Records for Bruce Walter Ogden-Smith.

HS 9/1377/2 – Records for Colin Malcolm Ogden-Smith.

HS 9/48/1 – Records for Geoffrey Appleyard.

HS 9/888/2 – Records for Anders Lassen.

TS 26/337 – United Nations War Crimes Commission – United Kingdom Charges against German War Criminals. Charge No UK–G/B159. British statement regarding deportations of British subjects from the Channel Islands in February 1943, following the raid on Sark.

WO 218/41 – War Diaries of No. 12 Commando. This thin folder contains almost nothing about the actual operations, merely noting that some of the men had taken part in Operation Basalt.

WO 311/105 – A thick folder full of documents concerning war crimes charges against Oberst Knackfuss and General Müller, and others, regarding deportations from the Channel Islands in September 1942 and February 1943.

La Société Sercquaise, Sark

The following include materials found in the archive of the Seigneur of Sark, held in the same location:

Tom Remfrey, seventeen folios regarding Sark and Channel Islands deportations.

Various maps, including maps of mines, and a map showing German place names instead of the English and French names that are usually used on the island.

Press cuttings from Dame Sibyl's collection.

Notebooks detailing menus for food served to the Germans and cooked by the owners of the Dixcart Hotel – including the meal served to Mrs Pittard on her return from Guernsey.

Richard Dewe has done a chronology of the years of German occupation, available here in typescript, with a very detailed account of the raid and its aftermath.

Guernsey newspapers from the period, which show the German propaganda line following the raid.

Early editions of the *La Trobe Guide to Sark* that were almost certainly used by Appleyard in planning the raid.

The translation into English of the chapter on the Sark raid in
Saelen's Norwegian-language biography of Anders Lassen –
sent to the Dame of Sark by the author.

Copies of postcards sent back to the island by the deportees
to Germany – including one from Mrs Pittard.

SECONDARY SOURCES

Appleyard, J.E.A., *Geoffrey: Major John Geoffrey Appleyard, Being
the Story of 'Apple' of the Commandos and Special Air Service
Regiment* (London: Blandford Press Ltd, 1946).

Aufsess, Baron von, *The von Aufsess Occupation Diary*, edited
and translated by Kathleen J. Nowland (Chichester:
Phillimore, 1985).

Bard, Robert, *The Channel Islands at War: A Dark History*
(Gloucestershire: Amberley Publishing, 2014).

Briggs, Asa, *History and Memory: The Case of the Channel Islands*
(Saint Helier: Société Jersiase, 1997).

Bunting, Madeleine, *The Model Occupation: The Channel Islands
Under German Rule* (London: Pimlico, 1995).

Carr, Gilly, Paul Sanders & Louise Willmot, *Protest, Defiance and
Resistance in the Channel Islands: German Occupation, 1940–
45* (London: Bloomsbury, 2014).

Cohen, Frederick, *The Jews in the Channel Islands During the
German Occupation* (Jersey: Jersey Heritage Trust, 2000).

Cruickshank, Charles, *The German Occupation of the Channel
Islands* (Stroud: Alan Sutton Publishing, 1990).

Durand, Ralph, *Guernsey Under German Rule* (London: The
Guernsey Society, 1946).

Ewen, A.H. and Allan R. De Carteret, *The Fief of Sark* (Guernsey:
Guernsey Press, 1969).

Falla, Frank, *The Silent War* (Guernsey: Burbridge, 1967).

Forty, George, *Channel Islands at War: A German Perspective*
(Shepperton: Ian Allan Publishing, 1999).

Fournier, Gérard and André Heintz, *'If I Must Die …' From 'Postmaster' to 'Aquatint'* (Cully, France: OREP Editions, 2006).

Fraser, David, *The Jews of the Channel Islands and the Rule of Law, 1940–1945* (Brighton: Sussex Academic Press, 2000).

Harris, Roger E., *Islanders Deported*, Part I (Ilford: C.I.S.S. Publishing, 1979).

Hathaway, Sibyl, *Dame of Sark: An Autobiography* (London: Heinemann, 1961).

Heaume, Richard, 'The Little Commandant of Sark', *Channel Islands Occupation Review*, No. 27, December 1999.

Hitler, Adolf, *Hitler's Table Talk* (London: Weidenfeld and Nicolson, 1953).

Jacobs, Peter, *Codenamed Dorset: The Wartime Exploits of Major Colin Ogden-Smith, Commando and SOE* (London: Frontline Books, 2014).

Keene, Tom, *Britain's Band of Brothers* (Stroud: The History Press, 2014).

Konstam, Angus, *British Motor Torpedo Boat 1939–45* (Oxford: Osprey, 2003).

Lassen, Suzanne, *Anders Lassen VC* (London: Frederick Muller Limited, 1965).

Le Feuvre, Nellie, *A Sark Teenager's Deportation* (privately printed, 2005).

Le Tissier, Richard, *Island Destiny: A True Story of Love and War in the Channel Island of Sark* (St Helier: Seaflower Books, 2006).

Le Tissier, Richard, *Mined Where You Walk: The German Occupation of Sark* (St Helier: Seaflower Books, 2008).

Lett, Brian, *The Small Scale Raiding Force* (London: Pen & Sword Military, 2013).

Lewis, Damien, *Churchill's Secret Warriors: The Explosive True Story of the Special Forces Desperadoes of WWII* (London: Quercus, 2014).

McLoughlin, Roy, *Living with the Enemy: An outline of the German Occupation of the Channel Islands with First-hand Accounts* by People who Remember the Years 1940 to 1945 (St John, Jersey: Channel Island Publishing, 1995).

Marshall, Michael, *Hitler Invaded Sark* (Guernsey: Paramount-Lithoprint, 1963).

Mayne, Richard, *Channel Islands Occupied: Unique Pictures of the Nazi Rule 1940–1945* (Norwich: Jarrold & Sons Limited, 1972).

Moreman, Tim, *British Commandos 1940–46* (Oxford: Osprey Publishing, 2006).

Nettles, John, *Jewels and Jackboots: Hitler's British Channel Islands* (Seeker Publishing, 2013).

Niven, David, *The Moon's a Balloon* (Magna Print Book, 1976).

Ramsey, Winston G., *The War in the Channel Islands: Then and Now* (London: After the Battle, 1981).

Saelen, Frithjof, *Unge Anders Lassen*. Text of the chapter on the Sark Raid translated by Miss Benedicte Laursen, Gothesgade, 1951.

Scotland, Lieutenant Colonel A.P., *The London Cage* (London: Evans Brothers Limited, 1957).

Stephenson, Charles, *The Channel Islands 1941–45: Hitler's Impregnable Fortress* (Oxford: Osprey, 2006).

Stokes, Peter, *No Ordinary Life* (FeedARead.com, 2013).

Tremayne, Julia, *War on Sark: The Secret Letters of Julia Tremayne* (Exeter: Webb & Bower, 1981).

Toms, Carel, *Hitler's Fortress Islands: Photo History of the German Occupation* (Four Square Book, 1967).

Wood, Alan and Mary, *Islands in Danger: The Story of the German Occupation of the Channel Islands, 1940–1945* (Morley: The Emfield Press, 1955).

ONLINE SOURCES

See http://www.operationbasalt.com for a full list.

ACKNOWLEDGEMENTS

Living in London has given me a great advantage in writing this book. I've had free and easy access to three great research institutions: the British Library, The National Archives and the Imperial War Museum. The first of these has been like a second home to me over many months and I am very grateful for the services offered by all three.

In Sark, I'd like to thank Dr Richard Axton and La Société Sercquaise for all their help, including access to their archives and the archives of the Seigneur. It was a great privilege to be able to address members of the Société and other local residents of Sark in February 2015. I was also able to interview three veterans of that period, Werner and Phyllis Rang and Esther Perree. I appreciate the assistance of Richard Dewe and Kevin Adams in helping to find photos and, in Richard's case, for first pointing me to the mysterious case of Major Skelton. Jeremy La Trobe-Bateman was very helpful as my guide, when we retraced the route taken by commandos.

In Guernsey, I was helped by Richard Heaume of the German Occupation Museum, and was also able to spend a most interesting afternoon using the Island Archives, which contain a great deal of material about Sark during the war.

I'd like to thank Doris Theuerkauf, the daughter of Oberleutnant Herdt, for her memories and photos. I want to thank the Deutsche Dienststelle für die Benachrichtigung der nächsten Angehörigen von Gefallenen der ehemaligen deutschen Wehrmacht (WASt) for providing me with Obergefreiter Hermann Weinreich's PWIB Form No. 2, which tells what happened to him after his capture by British commandos.

Peter Stokes and Graham Robinson, the sons of Sergeant Horace 'Stokey' Stokes and Sergeant Joseph Henry 'Tim' Robinson, generously shared their memories.

Thanks also to authors Peter Jacobs, for sharing material from Colin Ogden-Smith's diary, and Brian Lett for answering several questions. Thanks also to Jak P. Mallmann Showell and Lawrence Paterson for sharing their expertise regarding MTB 344 and answering my questions.

In Dorset, Jeremy and Rosemary Isaac kindly showed me around the gardens and the chapel at Anderson Manor, telling me what they had learned over the years about the commandos who stayed there. Phillip Ventham, a local historian in the area and the organiser of the 1988 meeting of the surviving commandos there, also gave some helpful pointers in my research.

I'm deeply in debt to all those who agreed to read this manuscript and for their helpful comments: Dr Richard Axton, Roger Darlington, Gary Kent, Martin Lee, Doerte Letzmann, John McCarthy and Dr Hilary Sapire.

I would like to thank the Authors' Foundation (Society of Authors) for their generous grant that made research on Sark possible.

Thanks also to Michael Leventhal at The History Press for taking this project on and for his enthusiastic support throughout.

Traditionally authors at this point thank their families for support, for tolerating them during their many months' long obsession with the subject of the book, and so on. I can now understand why. It was in conversation with my partner Cindy Berman that I first came up with the idea for this book while wandering along Sark's beautiful clifftop paths. Little did she know that it would mean walls in our home covered with Post-it notes about Operation Basalt, a huge wall map of Sark, and photos of the various commandos (including a particularly mean-looking Anders Lassen). Appleyard and his men, the Dame of Sark, Mrs Pittard, even 'Little Steve' all became part of our family for the last few months, ever present in our discussions and our lives. I hope it was worth it.

INDEX OF NAMES

INDEX OF NAMES